RACQUETBALL

MASTERING THE BASICS WITH THE PERSONALIZED SPORTS INSTRUCTION SYSTEM

Michael Metzler
Georgia State University

Allyn and Bacon

Boston   London   Toronto   Sydney   Tokyo   Singapore

VICE PRESIDENT	Paul A. Smith
PUBLISHER	Joseph E. Burns
EDITORIAL ASSISTANT	Annemarie Kennedy
MARKETING MANAGER	Rick Muhr
EDITORIAL PRODUCTION SERVICE	Bernadine Richey Publishing Services
TEXT DESIGN AND COMPOSITION	Barbara Bert Silbert
MANUFACTURING BUYER	Julie McNeill
COVER ADMINISTRATOR	Brian Gogolin

Copyright ©2001 by Allyn & Bacon
A Pearson Education Company
160 Gould Street
Needham Heights, MA 02494

Internet: www.abacon.com

ISBN: 0-205-32372-3

Printed in the United States of America

10 9 8 7 6 5 4 3 2 1   05 04 03 02 01 00

CONTENTS

PREFACE

INTRODUCTION TO PSIS RACQUETBALL

Hello, and welcome to your **racquetball class**! That's right, *your* racquetball class. This personal workbook includes almost everything you will need to learn the game of racquetball and become a proficient beginning-level player. Of course, your instructor will play an important part as you progress, but most of what you will need is contained in your Personal Workbook. Your racquetball class will be taught this term using the **Personalized Sports Instruction System (PSIS)**, developed specifically for college basic instruction courses like the one in which you are enrolled. All of the materials in this workbook have been refined in field tests with many students like yourself, college men and women getting their first formal racquetball instruction.

The key design feature of the PSIS is that it allows for individualized learning and progression through the course. Think back to other classes you have taken; some students learn faster than others. This is a fact in all learning situations. Depending on individual learning rates, some students become frustrated if the course goes too fast. Others become bored if the course goes too slowly. Either way, many students become disinterested, reducing their enjoyment of the course. For racquetball, the most harmful result of frustration or boredom is that students are not given a proper chance to learn the game and to enjoy it as a regular part of their activity schedule. Whether you are a "bare beginner" or currently have some racquetball experience, the PSIS design will allow you to progress **"as quickly as you can, or as slowly as you need."** Keep this little motto in mind as you become familiar with this workbook and progress through your racquetball class this term.

Another point to keep in mind is that the PSIS is *achievement oriented*. This means that the PSIS design is intended to help you learn the necessary skills, strategies, and rules for beginning racquetball play. We guarantee you will be a better player at the end of your PSIS class than you are now!

As you will see, your improvement will come in a way that is different from most other courses you have taken. You will be asked to assume more responsibility for your own learning than ever before. Remember, all the instructional material is included in your Personal Workbook. It will be up to you to learn the contents of the workbook, become familiar with the PSIS system, attend class regularly, follow your instructor's class policies, and work diligently toward completing the course sequences. It has been our experience that college students enjoy taking a large role in their own learning and appreciate the individualized plan of the PSIS. I know that you will, too.

ADVANTAGES OF THE PSIS FOR YOU

1. **The PSIS reduces your dependence on the instructor**. Your Personal Workbook provides nearly all the information you will need to complete the

course. All content, learning task, and managerial information is at your fingertips, not with the instructor. When you are ready for a new learning task, the individualized plan will allow you to proceed on your own.

2. **Individualized learning is emphasized.** The PSIS will allow you to learn racquetball "as quickly as you can, or as slowly as you need." You will be able to remain in your own comfort zone while progressing through the course.

3. **You will have increased responsibility for your own learning.** As adult learners, college students can assume responsibility for much of their own learning. You can make decisions that have direct bearing on class attendance, practice routines, and achievement. The PSIS system shifts much of the responsibility and decision making directly to you and away from the instructor.

4. **Your access to the instructor will be increased whenever you need it.** Since PSIS instructors can spend much more time in class teaching students, it means that you will get more personal attention and quality instruction, *that is, if you need it.* If you do not require as much interaction with the instructor, it will not be forced on you as with group learning strategies.

5. **You can chart your own progress.** Your PSIS Racquetball Personal Workbook includes a simple **Personal Progress Chart** to help you gauge your learning as you go through the course. This will help you to make decisions about your learning pace, projected grade, and how to use your class time most efficiently.

YOUR ROLE IN PSIS RACQUETBALL

Your role in PSIS racquetball can be summarized easily: become familiar with and follow the Personal Workbook as an independent learning guide. You will not need to depend on the instructor for content and managerial information. But when the workbook is not sufficient or specific learning information is needed, you should be sure to *ASK FOR HELP*! Your Personal Workbook will provide nearly all the information needed to complete the course. So, if you can progress without the instructor's direction, the system is designed to let you. If you need help, the instructor will be free to provide it for you. Your instructor will show you a *help signal* for getting his or her attention in class. It might be a raised hand, a raised racquet, or a verbal call. Be sure you know this signal, and do not be shy about using it!

YOUR INSTRUCTOR'S ROLE IN PSIS RACQUETBALL

Your instructor has the important role of *facilitator* in your PSIS racquetball course. Your Personal Workbook will provide most of the content and management information you will need, providing your instructor more time to give students individual attention. There will be just one large-group demonstration throughout the entire course, and very little time will be spent organizing routine class "chores." Nearly all the instructor's time will be available to facilitate your learning on an individual basis.

Your instructor has the teaching experience and expertise to make the PSIS work as well as it was designed. The PSIS system allows the instructor to provide the maximum use of his or her expertise by *facilitating* the learning process for you.

SKILL AND KNOWLEDGE COURSE MODULES

Your PSIS racquetball course contains a number of learning activities divided into a series of modules. There are two types of modules: **performance skill** and **rac-**

quetball knowledge. Performance skill modules focus on the major psychomotor performance patterns needed to play racquetball. The racquetball knowledge module contains information on basic game rules and racquetball etiquette.

PSIS COURSE MANAGEMENT AND POLICIES

In this section you will learn some of the ways in which the PSIS approach can give you increased control over your own learning. Some course management and policies will come from your Personal Workbook. Others will be communicated to you by your instructor. Be sure that you are familiar with all course management routines and policies.

1. **Dressing for class.** You will need to have proper clothing and footwear in order to participate comfortably and safely in your racquetball class. We suggest that you wear lightweight, loose-fitting clothes that will not restrict your range of motion (shorts, T-shirts, and the like). General-purpose court shoes or "cross training" shoes with white soles are recommended. Do not wear running shoes or shoes that will make marks on the floor. Specialized clothing and racquetball shoes are not necessary. Be sure to ask your instructor about his or her policies regarding dressing for class.

2. **Equipment.** Your instructor will provide you with all the necessary equipment for class and the routines for distributing and collecting equipment each day.

3. **Depositing and distributing Personal Workbooks.** Your instructor will advise you on his or her policy regarding your workbook each day after class. We suggest that the instructor collect all student workbooks at the end of class and bring them to class the next day. Be sure that you know the exact policy to be used, since you cannot participate fully in class without your own workbook.

4. **Practice partners.** Some learning tasks will call for you to practice with one or more partners and be checked off by them. Any classmate can be your partner for most tasks. A few tasks will specify that all students in a drill be at the same place in the course learning sequence.

5. **Arriving to class** Your instructor will inform you about specific routines for arriving to class and beginning each day. Generally, you should (1) arrive at or before the class starting time, (2) locate your own Personal Workbook, (3) complete your stretching and warm-up routine, (4) find a practice partner (if needed at that time), and (5) begin to practice the appropriate learning task. Note that you can begin as soon as you arrive. Except for the first day of instruction, the instructor will not wait to begin the class with all students together. *Arriving before class will allow you extra time to practice your racquetball skills.*

6. **Self-checks, partner checks, and instructor checks.** Each learning task in PSIS racquetball requires that your mastery be documented (checked off). Some tasks can be checked off by you, some must be checked off by a partner, and others by your instructor. Items are checked off by the appropriate person initialing and dating the designated area after each checked task in your Personal Workbook. Instructor-checked tasks will require that you practice for a period of time prior to attempting mastery and being checked off. When you are ready, indicated by a series of successful trial blocks, signal the instruc-

tor and ask him or her to observe you. If you do not reach the stated criterion, you can return for more practice and signal for the instructor again at a later time. *There is no penalty for not making a mastery criterion. You can try as many times as it takes to be successful.* You may find it helpful to alert the instructor at the beginning of a class in which you anticipate needing his or her observation and checking. The instructor will then be on the lookout for your signal.

7. **Grading.** Your course instructor will inform you about the grading system and related policies to be used in your PSIS racquetball class. Be sure you are aware of the specific requirements and procedures for determining your grade.

USING YOUR TIME EFFECTIVELY

Your PSIS racquetball course is made up of a series of predetermined learning tasks grouped into ten modules. Your course will have a set number of class days with a set class length. It is important for you to know your own learning pace and to make steady progress toward completing all course requirements. Therefore, you will need to learn how to best use your time in class and to accurately project completion of PSIS racquetball before the end of the term. Here are some helpful tips for managing your time.

1. Arrive to class early and begin right away. No signal will be given by the instructor for class to begin.
2. Stay for the entire class period. Do not get into the habit of leaving early.
3. Learn the PSIS course management system right away. The quicker you understand how it works, the sooner you can start using it to your advantage.
4. Do not hesitate to ask the instructor for assistance. Learn and use the class help signal to get the instructor's attention.
5. If there is not enough time to complete a new task in a class, at least *start* it. This will save time the next day.
6. When you are close to finishing a task at the end of a class, try to stay a few minutes late to complete it. This avoids repetitious setup time the next day and the possible loss of your learning momentum.
7. When a practice partner is needed, pair up with the first person you can find, rather than waiting for a certain person. (This is good way to get to know more of your classmates!)
8. Alert the instructor prior to instructor-checked criterion tasks so that she or he is available when you need observation and a check-off.

PSIS RACQUETBALL LEARNING MODULES

This section will describe how the PSIS course learning modules are designed. It is important that you know how the PSIS works so that you can take advantage of its individualized learning features. The course learning content is included in two kinds of learning modules: **performance skill** and **racquetball knowledge**.

Each *performance skill* module will include the following:
1. A written **introduction** to the skill
2. An **instructor demonstration** of the proper skill techniques
3. Text and photographs that explain the **components** or **phases** of each skill

4. Photographs that highlight the key **performance cues** (these same cues will be presented by the instructor in his or her demonstration).
5. Simple **comprehension tasks** and **readiness drills** to develop initial skill patterns
6. An **error analysis** and **correction section** for self-analyzing common mistakes
7. **Learning tips** for increased proficiency
8. A series of several **criterion tasks** for practicing and demonstrating your skill mastery
9. One or more **challenge tasks** for developing tactical applications of skills in modified competitive situations
10. A **Personal Recording Form** for selected tasks, used to record successful practice trials

The *racquetball knowledge* module will include:

1. A **reading** on the basic rules of racquetball and racquetball game strategy
2. A **knowledge quiz** to test your understanding of the rules and strategy

CHARTING YOUR PROGRESS

The last page of your PSIS racquetball workbook includes your **Personal Progress Chart**. Your instructor will show you how to correctly label the chart, and the rest is very simple. At the end of each week in the course, put an X above that date and across from the last task you completed. As the weeks go by, you will begin to see how your individual learning pace projects your successful completion of all course learning tasks.

This introductory section, combined with additional information from your instructor, will allow you to use the PSIS racquetball workbook to your full advantage and to learning racquetball at your own pace with highly individualized attention from your instructor. Because PSIS racquetball is a complete system for learning the game, it might take you a little time to become familiar with this approach. However, remember that your instructor is there to help when you have questions about the system and when you need individual attention for learning. Now that you know about the PSIS racquetball system, you are probably anxious to get started. We hope you enjoy learning racquetball with the PSIS approach and that you will become an avid player of this lifelong game.

READY...SET...GO!!

MODULE 1

STRETCHING FOR RACQUETBALL

INTRODUCTION

Flexibility refers to the ability of the muscles, tendons, and ligaments around a joint to move while providing support and allowing the joint to move smoothly through its entire range of motion. Increased flexibility means more supple muscles, which reduces the risk of injury to the muscle when the limb is moved suddenly. The static method is the most commonly recommended stretching technique. It has been shown to be extremely effective in increasing range of motion and, when done slowly and carefully, presents little chance of injury to the muscles.

Some sports and forms of exercise lead to improved flexibility of the involved body part. Racquetball, for example, tends to limber the shoulder joint and lower back. Gymnastics can only be accomplished with a high degree of flexibility in virtually all points of the body. Activities such as walking and jogging do not require a large range of motion and do not increase flexibility. This is why it is important that stretching should precede these types of exercises. Stretching not only enhances performance, but also reduces the risk of injury.

Flexibility should be included during the warm-up phase of an exercise program. This permits for gentle stretching of muscles around the joint before vigorous movement and leads to a slower cool-down, thereby maintaining local blood flow and reducing postexercise soreness.

Although muscular soreness can have many origins, one major cause appears to be damage to the connective tissue elements in the muscles and tendons. No one method of overcoming soreness is available, but adequate stretching appears to aid not only in preventing soreness but also in relieving it when it already exists.

PERFORMANCE CUES

1. **Warm-up.** Protect the muscle by beginning with a- low to moderate-intensity warm-up for 2 to 3 minutes prior to performing strenuous stretching exercises. Running in place should provide an excellent warm-up.
2. **Do not bounce.** Move into the stretching position slowly, continuing until mild tension is felt. Utilize a static or very slow stretch and hold the position. A ballistic or bouncing stretch can be counterproductive and even cause injury.
3. **Hold the stretch.** The stretch position should be held for a predetermined amount of time. It is suggested that the initial holding position be between 15 and 20 seconds and be gradually increased over the following weeks. As flexibility improves, attempt to hold the stretch slightly longer. When the stretching exercise is complete, the body should be released slowly from the stretch position.
4. **Target Zone.** You should not feel pain when stretching a muscle. There is a stretching target zone where *there is tension in the muscle without pain*. It is important to be aware of your own target zone. Stretching at a level below the target zone will not lead to increased flexibility, whereas stretching above this zone will increase the risk of injury.
5. **Breathing.** Do not hold your breath while stretching. Breathing should be slow, rhythmical, and continuous.
6. **Stretch before and after exercise.** Stretching before vigorous exercise prepares the muscles and joint for activity and reduces the risk of injury. Stretching after vigorous exercise is needed to further stretch the muscles. Both warm-up and cool-down are needed.

INSTRUCTOR DEMONSTRATION

Your course instructor will demonstrate each of the recommended stretching exercise for racquetball. Observe the demonstration carefully, making note of the performance cues for each exercise.

Shoulder Stretch (triceps) Elevate one elbow and position the racquet down the middle of your back. Reach behind your back with the other hand and grab the racquet slightly above belt-high. Gently apply force by moving the non-racquet hand down, causing your other elbow to rise (and stretch). Hold

Photo 1.1
Shoulder Stretch

the stretch in the target zone for 15 to 20 seconds and slowly release. Repeat this exercise 5 to 8 times with both shoulders. Refer to Photo 1.1.

Lateral shoulder stretch Elevate the arms and grip the racquet at each end. Gently pull down with one arm, stretching the opposite shoulder. Bend your hips in the direction of the pull. Knees should be slightly flexed during the exercise. Hold the stretch in the target zone for 15 to 20 seconds and slowly release. Repeat this exercise 5 to 8 times on both sides of the body. Refer to Photo 1.2.

Lower back and hamstrings stretch From a standing position and holding the racquet at each end, bend forward at the hips and allow the head and arms to hang downward. Have both knees slightly flexed during this exercise. Hold the stretch in the target zone for 15 to 20 seconds and slowly release. Repeat this exercise 5 to 8 times. Refer to Photo 1.3.

Lower back and hip extensor stretch From a supine position, elevate one leg toward your chest. Apply pressure for the stretch with both arms pulling toward the chest. Hold the stretch in the target zone for 15 to 20 seconds and slowly release. Repeat this exercise 5 to 8 times with each leg. Refer to Photo 1.4

Photo 1.2
Lateral Shoulder Stretch

Photo 1.3
Lower Back and
Hamstrings Stretch

Photo 1.4
Lower Back and Hip Extensor Stretch

Wall stretch (gastrocnemius) Take a position 2 to 3 feet from a wall or solid structure. Lean forward and support your body weight with your forearms. Flex one leg and position the other leg to the rear with the front foot flat on the floor. Force your hips forward while keeping the back leg straight. Hold

Photo 1.5
Wall Stretch

the stretch in the target zone for 15 to 20 seconds and slowly release. Repeat this exercise 5 to 8 times with each leg. Refer to Photo 1.5

CRITERION TASK 1-1

Performing Stretches: Partner-Checked

Pair up with another person in the class. In turn, perform each stretch while the partner observes for proper technique. Have your partner check and initial below when you have performed each stretch just as your instructor demonstrated. If you have questions or need assistance, use the help signal to alert your instructor.

1. Shoulder stretch
2. Lateral shoulder stretch
3. Lower back and hamstrings stretch
4. Lower back and hip extensor stretch
5. Wall stretch

Your partner's initials _____ Date completed _____

MODULE 2

RACQUETBALL BASICS

INTRODUCTION

Racquetball is a fast-paced game that requires a combination of skill, positioning, and strategy. Once in play, the ball moves very fast and must carom off the front wall before it can be struck again. The fast movement of the ball calls for players to anticipate where it will go and to move to a place on the court to make the proper shot, at the same time considering the position of the opponent. Tactically, the game is very simple: try to hit a shot that your opponent cannot return before the ball hits the court twice. However, the speed at which the ball moves, the possibility of multiple wall contacts, and the relatively small size of the court make this tactical goal difficult to achieve when playing against an evenly matched opponent.

Even the best racquetball players started out as beginners, and they still understand one thing about how to play the game: it all starts with the several basic skills that must be mastered before moving to more advanced levels of play. This module will introduce you to the fundamentals of racquetball and give you a strong start on building the skills and knowledge that must be applied to all aspects of the game.

EQUIPMENT

Racquetball requires little equipment to play, one reason for its popularity in so many countries. Racquetball equipment is relatively inexpensive and durable. The basic design of the two most essential pieces of equipment, the racquet and the ball, has changed little in recent years. The few changes that have occurred are in the materials used for racquets and the liveliness of the ball.

7

THE RACQUET

The striking implement, or racquet, used to play racquetball is lightweight and thin. The body of the racquet is usually made of a fiber-glass composite material, and the strings are made of thin nylon cord. The handle grip is commonly wrapped with a thin layer of leather. A wrist lanyard is anchored from the bottom of the handle; it is used as a safety device to prevent the racquet from accidentally flying out of your hand. Your instructor will show you how to use the wrist lanyard properly. It is a good idea not only to check your own use of the lanyard, but also to be sure that all other players on the court with you are using theirs properly as well.

THE BALL

Modern racquetballs are made of a rubberlike vinyl compound. They are hollow, with a thin skin covered with a tacky surface. This tackiness serves two purposes. It helps the ball grip the floor and wall surfaces for truer bounces, and once the tackiness wears off it indicates that it is time for a new ball.

SHOES AND ATTIRE

It is important that you have the proper shoes for playing racquetball to increase comfort and safety. It is not important at this time to have shoes designed specifically for racquetball. Shoes rated for general indoor court use or cross training will work well. *Running shoes are not recommended because of their narrow soles and limited ankle support*. Finally, make sure your shoes have white soles, not black, so that they will not mark the court. Your attire should include socks, shorts, and a lightweight short-sleeved shirt. Your shorts and shirt should allow for a comfortable, full range of motion and provide good ventilation. Racquetball is a very active game and your clothing should allow your body to easily evaporate perspiration. But be careful that your clothing is not too loose; if the ball touches any part of your clothing, it counts as touching you, which is a violation.

EYE PROTECTORS

All players should wear eye protectors rated for use in racquetball. To prevent eye injuries from the ball these should be worn even when you are the only person practicing on the court. Just as you should wear eye protectors, you should not play racquetball with any others who are not wearing adequate eye protection.

COURT

COURT LAYOUT

It is important that racquetball players know the layout of the court. Not only does the layout define boundaries for serves and other shots, it is also used to describe court positioning and shot placement. Illustration 2.1 is a diagram of the racquetball court and its various lines and boundaries.

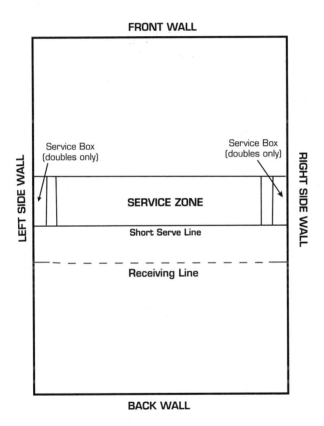

Illustration 2.1
Court and zone lines

COMPREHENSION TASK

Study Illustration 2.1 until you can identify all the labeled lines on the diagram. Then have a partner call out the names of the various parts of the racquetball court. After each part is called, walk onto the court and either stand on or point to that part. Repeat this task until you correctly identify every line or area with no mistakes.

RACQUETBALL FUNDAMENTALS

Racquetball is a game is which the little things count, because the ball moves at a very high speed and even minor mistakes or indecisions can cause you to lose a point. These little things include several fundamentals that all beginning players should know and use at all times. The most basic skill in racquetball is the **ready position**, which allows the player to move in every direction on the court quickly and equally well. During competition you will not know where the shot will go until it leaves your opponent's racquet, so it is important to be in a good ready position to move quickly in all directions. Refer to Photo 2.1 as you read the performance cues for the ready position.

Photo 2.1
Ready position

READY POSITION

1. Your feet should be slightly more than shoulder-width apart, with both feet turned slightly outward.
2. Your knees should bend slightly. Do not lock them into one position.
3. Bend forward at the waist until your heels start to come off the floor, giving you a "floating" weight distribution.
4. Position the racquet in front of you, with the handle at waist height. Do not favor the forehand or backhand sides with your racquet position.

FOREHAND GRIP

The term **grip** refers to how the hand fits around the grip of the racquet. Ball direction and power are both related to the type of grip used during the stroke. There are two basic grips that most players use, the **forehand grip** and the **backhand grip**. The forehand grip is used to make shots from your dominant side (the side holding the racquet).

INSTRUCTOR DEMONSTRATION

Your course instructor will explain and demonstrate the key performance cues for the forehand grip. If you have questions, be sure to ask them before proceeding to the individualized task sequence. Refer to Photo 2.2 as your instructor explains and demonstrates the performance cues for this grip.

PERFORMANCE CUES

1. **Thumb** and **index finger** form a V that is positioned on top of the grip.
2. **Index finger** (sometimes called the trigger finger) is wrapped around the grip and is separated from the middle finger.
3. **Thumb** is positioned down and around the grip and is in contact with the middle finger.
4. **Heel** of the hand is in contact with the base of the grip.
5. **Forearm** and racquet shaft form an angle of approximately 135 degrees.

READINESS DRILLS

2-1. **Find a partner.** Hold the racquet face perpendicular to the court. Have your partner "shake hands" with the grip of the racquet and assume the proper forehand grip. Use the performance cues to decide if his or her grip is correct. Switch roles and repeat this drill. Repeat this drill twice.
2-2. **Forehand dribble bounce.** Assume the forehand grip. Drop a ball onto the court and, as the ball rebounds, hit the ball back to the court.

Photo 2.2
Forehand Grip

Photo 2.3
Forehand dribble bounce

Continue bouncing the ball using the forehand face of the racquet (see Photo 2.3). Your score is the number of times the ball strikes the court. Your specific task, is to keep the ball in play for at least 20 consecutive bounces. To complete this task you must be successful in two sets of 20 consecutive hits.

2-3.   **Forehand air-bounce.** Assume the forehand grip. Toss the ball into the air and gently hit with the racquet. Keep the ball in the air rebounding off the forehand face of the racquet, about head-high (see Photo 2.4). The score is the number of times the ball strikes the forehand face of the racquet. Your task is to keep the ball in play for at least 20 consecutive hits. To complete this task, you must be successful in two sets of 20 consecutive hits.

If you experience difficulty with the readiness drills, refer to the **performance cues** and review each cue as presented. If you still have difficulty, ask your course instructor to assist you in applying these techniques.

Photo 2.4
Forehand air-bounce

Photo 2.5
Backhand grip

BACKHAND GRIP

A different grip is used for shots made from your backhand (nondominant) side. A slight adjustment must be made from the forehand grip to make the ball stay on the intended line and trajectory for backhand shots.

INSTRUCTOR DEMONSTRATION

Your course instructor will explain and demonstrate the key performance cue for the backhand grip. If you have questions, be sure to ask them before proceeding to the individualized task sequence. Refer to Photo 2.5 as your instructor explains and demonstrates each performance cue for this grip.

PERFORMANCE CUES

1. **Thumb** and **index finger** form a V that is positioned over the left beveled top edge (as you look down) of the racquet.
2. **Index finger** (sometimes called the trigger finger) is wrapped around the grip and is separated from the middle finger.
3. **Thumb** is positioned down (approximately 45 degrees) and around the grip and is out of contact with the middle finger. The side of the thumb braces the back of the racquet.
4. **Heel** of the hand is firmly in contact with the base of the grip.
5. **Forearm** and racquet shaft form an angle of approximately 135 degrees.

READINESS DRILLS

2-4. **Backhand air-bounce.** Assume the backhand grip. Toss the ball into the air and gently hit it with the racquet. Keep the ball in the air rebounding off the backhand face of the racquet, about head-high (see Photo 2.6). The score is the number of times the ball strikes the backhand face of the racquet. Your task is to keep the ball in play for at least 20 consecutive hits. To complete this task, you must be successful in two sets of 20 consecutive hits.

Photo 2.6
Backhand air-bounce

2-5.   **Alternating forehand-backhand air-bounce.**   Assume the forehand grip. Toss the ball into the air and gently hit it with the forehand face of the racquet. Use the backhand face to execute the next hit. Alternate between the forehand and backhand faces to keep the ball in the air (see Photo 2.7A and 2.7B). Do not try to change grips! The score is the number of consecutive times the ball strikes the racquet. Your task is to keep the ball in play for at least 20 consecutive hits. To complete this task, you must be successful in two sets of 20 consecutive hits.

If you experience difficulty with the readiness drills, refer to the **performance cues** and review each cue as presented. If you still have difficulty, ask your course instructor to assist you in applying these techniques.

Photo 2.7A
Forehand air-bounce

Photo 2.7B
Backhand air-bounce

LEARNING TIPS

1. Grip the racquet in a firm manner; but not too tight.
2. Relax the grip between shots.
3. Experiment with slight variations of the suggested grip styles.
4. Some players choose to hit both the forehand and the backhand with the *backhand* grip.

FOOTWORK

Footwork is important in racquetball, allowing you to move to the ball quickly and to strike the ball with maximum power. There are three basic footwork skills to master: the ready position, forehand, and backhand.

You can use the face of a clock to visualize the proper footwork for the **ready position**, forehand, and backhand shots. Refer to Illustration 2.2 which shows the foot placement for the ready position. The left foot is at 9 o'clock and the right foot is at 3 o'clock (as if you were looking directly down from above the player). Illustration 2.3 shows the foot placement for **forehand** shots (right-handed players). In the correct position for forehand shots, the right (back) foot is between 4 and 5 o'clock and the left (front) foot is at 1 o'clock. Illustration 2.4 shows the foot placement for **backhand** shots (right-handed players). In the correct position for backhand shots, the left (back) foot is between 7 and 8 o'clock and the right (front) foot is at 11 o'clock.

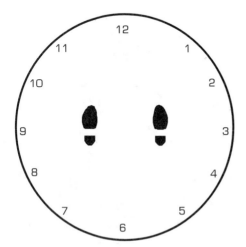

Illustration 2.2
Ready position footwork

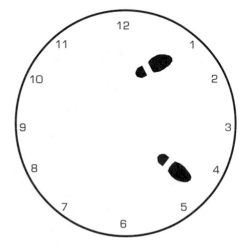

Illustration 2.3
Forehand footwork (right-handed)

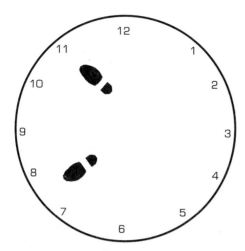

Illustration 2.4
Backhand footwork (right-handed)

COMPREHENSION TASK

Demonstrate to a partner the ready position with all the correct performance cues. While in the correct ready position, have your partner randomly call out "forehand" or "backhand." You should quickly execute the correct footwork and grip for the designated shot. Hold your position and have your partner check for correct execution. Be sure to return to the ready position before the next call is made. Do this 10 times and then switch roles with your partner.

CHALLENGE TASK

Front Wall Rally

Take a position a few feet behind the receiving line in the center of the court (X) (see Illustration 2.5). Drop the ball to the court. On the first bounce of the ball, stroke it to the front wall. Use both forehand and backhand strokes to keep the ball in play for at least 10 consecutive hits. The ball can be played on the fly or on the first bounce each time. If the ball takes more than two bounces between hits *or does not hit the front wall first after being struck*, you must start over. To complete this task, you must complete three sets of 10 consecutive hits.

Date completed _____

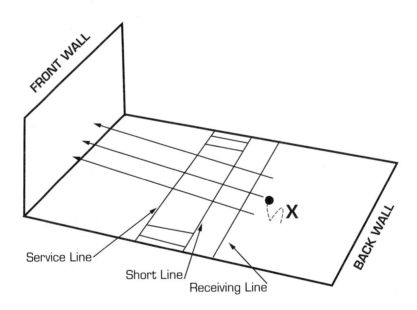

Illustration 2.5
Front wall rally

MODULE 3

FOREHAND STROKE

INTRODUCTION

The forehand is considered the basic stroke of racquetball. The forehand stroke is hit from the dominant-hand side of your body (your racquet side). Most racquetball players, including professionals, feel that it is their most dependable and powerful weapon. The forehand is also used to serve the ball. The basic forehand involves three phases: preparation (preparing to hit the ball), contact (contacting the ball), and follow-through (stroke pattern after ball contact).

INSTRUCTOR DEMONSTRATION

Your course instructor will demonstrate the key performance cues for the forehand stroke. If you have questions, be sure to ask them before proceeding to the individualized task sequence. Refer to Photos 3.1A through 3.1C as your instructor explains and demonstrates each of the performance cues for this skill.

PERFORMANCE CUES (PREPARATION)

1. **Grip:** Forehand grip
2. **Backswing:** Looping swing above the level of the shoulders.
3. **Foot pivot:** Body weight shifts to the rear foot, allowing the body to pivot sideways.
4. **Body rotation:** Hip and shoulders rotate clockwise, placing the side of the body toward the front wall.

PERFORMANCE CUES (CONTACT)

1. **Body weight transfer:** Take a short step forward with the lead foot. Body weight is shifted from the rear foot to the front foot.

Photo 3.1A
Forehand stroke,
backswing

Photo 3.1B
Forehand stroke,
contact

Photo 3.1C
Forehand stroke,
follow-through

2. **Ball contact:** Just forward of the lead foot.
3. **Wrist:** Rotates with the forearm to provide power.

PERFORMANCE CUES (Follow-through)

1. **Body rotation:** Hip and shoulders rotate counterclockwise.
2. **Forward swing:** Upward and across the body. Keep the follow-through compact so that you do not hit or interfere with another player on the court

COMPREHENSION TASK

Find a partner and take turns. Execute the forehand at nearly full speed, *without hitting the ball*, until you feel comfortable with the stroke. Have your court partner use the **Performance Cues** to decide if your forehand form is correct. Then switch roles and repeat this drill. Repeat this drill three times.

LEARNING TIPS

1. Move to anticipated ball contact spot as soon as possible.
2. Start the backswing early using a loop swing.
3. The racquet is parallel with the court at the top of the loop swing.
4. The knees are flexed to lower the center of gravity.
5. Hip and shoulder rotation turns the nondominant side of the body toward the front wall.
6. Body weight shifts forward toward the front wall.
7. At the point of ball impact, rotate the wrist and forearm to add power to the stroke.
8. Contact the ball with the arm extended. Do not let the ball get too close to your body.
9. Follow-through is across your body, elevated, and compact.

READINESS DRILL

3-1. **Drop-and-hit drill.** Take the court position a few feet behind the receiving line in the center of the court (X) (See Illustration 3.1). Drop a ball to the court. As the ball bounces from the floor, get into position and stroke it to the front wall with a *controlled* forehand drive. Do not attempt to volley at this time. The flight of the ball should be in a straight line (parallel with the side wall), and the ball should hit the front wall first. Repeat this drill 20 times.

If you experience difficulty with the readiness drill, refer to the **performance cues** and review each cue as presented. If you still have difficulty, ask your course instructor to assist you in applying these techniques.

Common Errors and Their Correction

Error	Correction
Ball drifts right into the side wall before hitting the front wall.	Adjust your ball contact forward toward the front wall.
Ball drifts across to the center of the court (crosscourt).	Adjust your ball contact backward toward the midline of your body.
Ball lacks velocity.	1. Transfer your body weight forward, into the point of ball contact. 2. Rotate your wrist and forearm forward during ball contact.

CRITERION TASK 3-1

Drop and Hit (Forehand): Self-Checked

Mark a line on the front wall 5 feet from the floor (see Illustration 3.1). Take the court position a few feet behind the receiving line in the center of the court (X). Drop the ball to the court. As the ball bounces from the floor, get into position and stroke it to the front wall with a **forehand drive**. The ball flight should travel in a straight line (parallel with the side wall), and the ball should hit the *front wall first*, below the marked line.

Practice this task in blocks of 10 serves. Record the number of successful shots for each block on the **Personal Recording Form**. When three block scores reach or exceed 8 out of 10, initial and date in the space provided.

Personal Recording Form									
Block 1	Block 2	Block 3	Block 4	Block 5	Block 6	Block 7	Block 8	Block 9	Block 10
___/10	___/10	___/10	___/10	___/10	___/10	___/10	___/10	___/10	___/10

Your initials _____　　Date completed _____

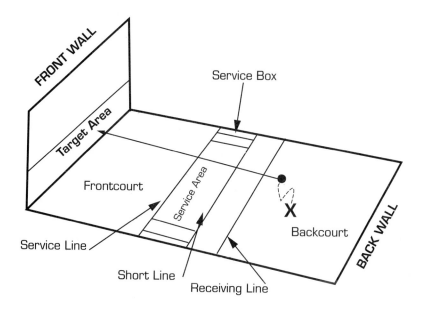

Illustration 3.1
Drop and hit (forehand)

CRITERION TASK 3-2

Side Wall Drop and Hit (Forehand): Instructor-Checked

Mark a line on the front wall 5 feet from the floor, and place a cone or other marker at the center of the front wall, forming a rectangle as your target (see Illustration 3.2). Take the court position a few feet behind the receiving line and 2 to 3 feet in from the right side wall (X) Gently toss the ball into the side wall at an angle of approximately 45 degrees. The rebound from the side wall should be well forward of the midline of your body. The ball should rebound from the floor only 1 to 2 feet from the level of the court. As the ball rebounds from the court, move into position and hit it with a forehand drive. The ball must not strike the side wall, floor, or ceiling before contact with the front wall, inside the marked rectangular target.

Practice this task in blocks of 10 shots. Record the number of successful shots in each block on the **Personal Recording Form**. When your block scores consistently reach or exceed 7, ask your instructor to observe and witness your attempt at criterion. Once your instructor has witnessed three successful blocks (7 of 10), have him or her initial and date in the space provided.

Personal Recording Form									
Block 1	Block 2	Block 3	Block 4	Block 5	Block 6	Block 7	Block 8	Block 9	Block 10
___/10	___/10	___/10	___/10	___/10	___/10	___/10	___/10	___/10	___/10

Instructor's initials _____   Date completed _____

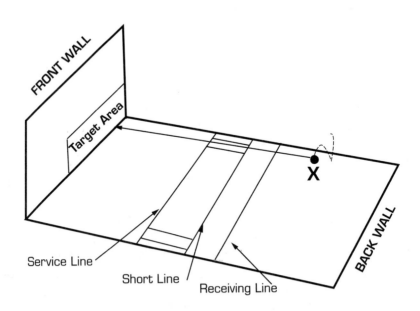

Illustration 3.2
Side wall drop and hit (forehand)

CHALLENGE TASK 3.1

Partner Rally (Be sure to wear your eyeguards)

Select a court partner and both players take positions in the backcourt. One player initiates a partner rally drill by stroking the ball to the front wall with a forehand drive. Both players attempt to keep the ball in play using only forehand drives. If the ball approaches the backhand, do not hit it. Allow the ball to continue its flight until it travels to a court position from which a player can execute a forehand drive. Allow the ball to contact any wall and/or ceiling and bounce an unlimited number of times. **The objective of this task is to keep the ball in play *as long as possible* using only forehand drives.** You may repeat this task as often as you wish.

CHALLENGE TASK 3.2

Drop and Hit Velocity Trials

Be sure to warmup before attempting this task. This challenge task is similar to Criterion Task 3-1, (drop and hit forehand), except the objective is maximum ball velocity. Take a court position a few feet behind the receiving line in the center of the court. Drop the ball to the court. As the ball bounces from the floor, get into position and stroke it to the front wall with a hard (high-velocity) forehand drive. **The objective of this task is to hit the ball *as hard as possible*, without the ball striking the side wall, floor or ceiling before contact with the front wall. The ball should hit the front wall below the marked 5-foot line.** You may repeat this task as often as you wish.

MODULE 4

BACKHAND STROKE

INTRODUCTION

The backhand stroke is made from the nondominant side of the body, across from the side on which you hold the racquet. The backhand drive consists of the same basic biomechanical components discussed in the forehand drive, with one modification. The grip recommended for the backhand drive is the backhand grip you learned in Module 2. The basic backhand involves three phases: preparation (preparing to hit the ball), contact (contacting the ball), and follow-through (stroke pattern after ball contact).

INSTRUCTOR DEMONSTRATION

Your course instructor will explain and demonstrate the key performance cues for the backhand stroke. If you have questions, be sure to ask them before proceeding to the individualized task sequence. Refer to Photos 4.1A through 4.1C as your instructor explains and demonstrates each performance cue for this skill.

PERFORMANCE CUES (Preparation)

1. **Grip:** Backhand grip
2. **Backswing:** Looping swing above the level of the shoulders.
3. **Body rotation:** Hip and shoulders rotate, placing the side of the body toward the front wall.

PERFORMANCE CUES (Contact)

1. **Body weight transfer:** Take a short step with the front foot. Body weight is shifted from the rear foot to the front foot.
2. **Ball contact:** Just forward of the front foot.
3. **Wrist:** Rotates with the forearm to provide power.

Photo 4.1A
Backhand stroke, back-swing

Photo 4.1B
Backhand stroke, contact

Photo 4.1AC
Backhand stroke, follow-through

PERFORMANCE CUES (Follow-through)

1. **Body rotation:** Hip and shoulders rotate clockwise.
2. **Forward swing:** Upward and across the body. Keep the follow-through compact so that you do not hit or interfere with another player on the court.

COMPREHENSION TASK

Find a partner and take turns. Execute the backhand at nearly full speed, *without hitting the ball*, until you feel comfortable with the stroke. Have your court partner use the **performance cues** to decide if your backhand form is correct. Then switch roles and repeat this drill. Repeat this drill 3 times.

LEARNING TIPS

1. Start the backswing early and move to the anticipated ball contact spot as soon as possible.
2. Use a loop swing.
3. Hip and shoulder rotation turns the side of your body toward the front wall.
4. Flex your knees to lower your center of gravity.
5. During ball impact, shift your body weight forward toward the front wall.
6. At the point of ball impact, rotate your wrist and forearm to add power to the stroke.
7. Contact the ball with your arm extended. Do not let the ball get too close to your body.
8. Follow-through across your body, elevated, and compact.

READINESS DRILL

4-1. **Drop-and-hit drill.** Take the court position a few feet behind the receiving line in the center of the court(X) (see Illustration 4.1). Drop a ball to the court. As the ball bounces from the floor, get into position and stroke it to the front wall with a *controlled* backhand drive. Do not attempt to volley at this time. The flight of the ball should be in a straight line (parallel with the side wall), and the ball should hit the front wall first. Repeat this drill 20 times.

   If you experience difficulty with the readiness drill, refer to the **performance cues** and review each cue as presented. If you still have difficulty, ask your course instructor to assist you in applying these techniques.

Common Errors and Their Correction

Error	Correction
Ball drifts left into the side wall before hitting the front wall.	Adjust your ball contact forward toward the front wall.
Ball drifts across the center of the court (crosscourt).	Adjust your ball contact backward toward the midline of your body.
Ball lacks velocity.	1. Transfer your body weight forward, into the point of ball contact.
	2. Rotate your wrist and forearm forward during ball contact.

CRITERION TASK 4-1

Drop and Hit (Backhand): Self-Checked

Mark a line on the front wall 5 feet from the floor. (see Illustration 4.1). Take the court position a few feet behind the receiving line in the center of the court (X). Drop the ball to the court on your backhand side. As the ball bounces from the floor, get into position and stroke it to the front wall with a **backhand drive**. The ball flight should travel in a straight line (parallel with the side wall), and the ball should hit the front wall first, below the marked line.

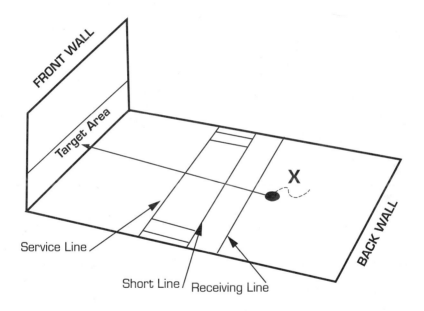

Illustration 4.1
Drop and hit (backhand)

Practice this task in blocks of 10 shots. Record the number of successful shots for each block on the **Personal Recording Form**. When three block scores reach or exceed 7 out of 10, initial and date in the space provided.

Personal Recording Form									
Block 1	Block 2	Block 3	Block 4	Block 5	Block 6	Block 7	Block 8	Block 9	Block 10
___/10	___/10	___/10	___/10	___/10	___/10	___/10	___/10	___/10	___/10

Your initials _____   Date completed _____

CRITERION TASK 4-2

Side Wall Drop and Hit (Backhand): Instructor-Checked

Mark a line on the front wall 5 feet from the floor and place a cone or other marker at the center of the front wall, forming a rectangle as your target (see Illustration 4.2). Take the court position a few feet behind the receiving line and 3 to 4 feet in from the side wall (X) Gently toss the ball into the side wall at an angle of approximately 45 degrees. The rebound from the side wall should be well forward of the mid-line of your body. The ball should rebound from the floor only 1–2 feet from the level of the court. As the ball rebounds from the court, move into position and return it with a backhand drive. The ball must not strike the side wall, floor, or ceiling before contact with the front wall, inside the marked rectangular target.

Practice this task in blocks of 10 shots. Record the number of successful shots in each block on the **Personal Recording Form**. When your block scores consistently reach or exceed 6, ask your instructor to observe and witness your attempt at criterion. Once your instructor has witnessed three successful blocks (6 of 10), have him or her initial and date in the space provided.

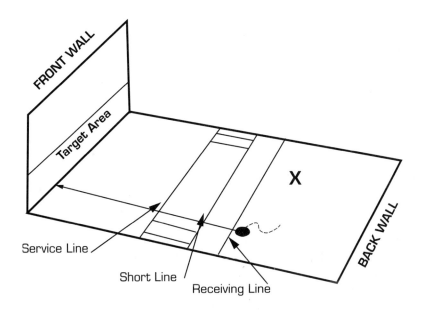

Illustration 4.2
Side wall drop and hit (backhand)

Personal Recording Form									
Block 1	Block 2	Block 3	Block 4	Block 5	Block 6	Block 7	Block 8	Block 9	Block 10
___/10	___/10	___/10	___/10	___/10	___/10	___/10	___/10	___/10	___/10

Instructor's initials _____   Date completed _____

CHALLENGE TASK

Partner Rally (Be sure to wear your eyeguards)

Select a court partner and both players take positions in the backcourt. One of the players initiates a partner rally drill by stroking the ball to the front wall with a backhand drive. Both players attempt to keep the ball in play using only backhand drives. If the ball approaches the forehand side, do not hit it. Allow the ball to continue its flight until it travels to a court position from which a player can execute a backhand drive. Allow the ball to contact any wall and/or ceiling, and bounce an unlimited number of times. **The objective of this task is to keep the ball in play** *as long as possible* **using only backhand drives.** You may repeat this task as often as you wish.

FOREHAND AND BACKHAND COMBINATIONS

INTRODUCTION

The speed of racquetball court play demands that a player be able to antici-pate and use both the forehand and backhand strokes, often alternating on every shot in a rally. It is important that you are able to interchange these shots and retain racquet control. Practicing these two shots as an integrated skill will improve your racquetball fundamentals.

READINESS DRILLS

4-2. Stand behind the receiving line. Drop the ball to the floor. As it rebounds, stroke it to the front wall with either a forehand or back-hand drive stroke. When it rebounds from the front wall, move into position and return the ball to the front wall again, using the forehand and backhand drive as necessary. *Play it on any bounce.* Do this as many times as you can without losing control of the ball. Stay behind the receiving line. Repeat this drill 10 times.

4-3. Find a partner and be sure that both of you are wearing your eye-guards. Both players stand near midcourt, one on each side of the cen-ter of the court. One player drops the ball to the floor and strokes it to the front wall with a medium-paced shot. When it rebounds from the front wall, the other player moves into position and returns the ball to the front wall, again using the forehand and backhand drive as necessary. *Play it on any bounce.* The object of this drill is to keep the ball in play as long as possible, using alternating shots by each player. Repeat this drill 10 times.

4-4. Find a partner and be sure that both of you are wearing your eyeguards. Both players stand near midcourt, one on each side of the center of the court. One player drops the ball to the floor and strokes it to the front wall with a medium-paced shot. When it rebounds from the front wall, the other player attempts to return it to the front wall *before it strikes the floor twice.* The drill continues until one player fails to return the ball. Repeat this drill 10 times.

CRITERION TASK 4-3

Multiple-bounce Rally: Self-Checked

Take the court position a few feet behind the receiving line (X) (see Illustration 4.3). Drop the ball to the floor. As it rebounds, stroke it to the front wall. When it rebounds from the front wall, move into position and return the ball to the front wall again with either forehand or backhand drive. *Play it on any bounce.* Use both forehand and backhand drives as necessary. Stay behind the receiving line.

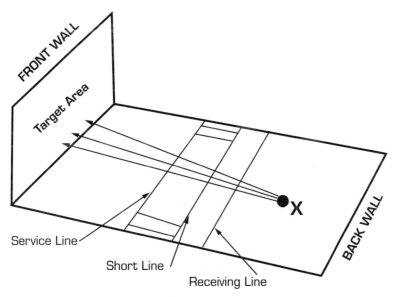

Illustration 4.3
Multiple-bounce rally

Record the number of successful shots for each attempt on the **Personal Recording Form**. When three scores reach at least 10 consecutive hits, initial and date in the space provided.

Personal Recording Form									
Block 1	Block 2	Block 3	Block 4	Block 5	Block 6	Block 7	Block 8	Block 9	Block 10
__/__	__/__	__/__	__/__	__/__	__/__	__/__	__/__	__/__	__/__

Your initials _____   Date completed _____

CHALLENGE TASK

Five-point Rally

Find a partner who has also completed Criterion Task 4-3. Make sure both players are wearing their eyeguards. Both players take the court position to the rear of the receiving line (see Illustration 4.4). Player A drops the ball and strokes it to the front wall so that the rebound will travel toward his or her court partner. When it rebounds from the front wall, player B attempts to return it to the front wall *before it strikes the floor twice*. The rally continues until one player fails to return the ball. The other player then has scored 1 point. Player B then puts the ball into play. Play continues until one player has scored 5 points. Repeat this for a total of seven games.

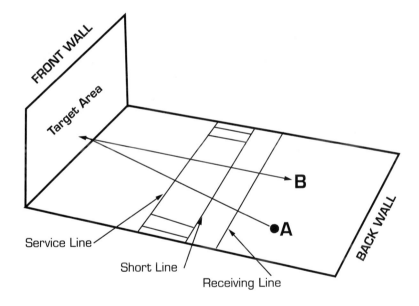

Illustration 4.4
Five-point rally

MODULE 5

BACK WALL STROKES

INTRODUCTION

One of racquetball's attractions is the speed at which the ball moves around the court. The speed of the ball, combined with the relatively small court size, often means that the ball will need to be played off the back wall during a rally. To become a skilled racquetball player, you must develop a strong back wall game, because these shots occur frequently during match play. Proper court position is extremely important when executing back wall shots. Novice players tend to chase after a ball that is moving from wall to wall rather than anticipating and moving to where the ball will eventually set up for the stroke. This is termed *reading the walls*. This skill will develop slowly over time with repeated play. In addition, many beginning players attempt to hit the ball before it reaches the back wall, not realizing that some bounces off the back wall can provide a player with the opportunity to hit a *kill shot*, the best offensive shot in the game.

FOREHAND BACK WALL STROKE

INSTRUCTOR DEMONSTRATION

Your course instructor will explain and demonstrate the key performance cues for the forehand back wall stroke. If you have questions, be sure to ask them before proceeding to the individualized task sequence. Refer to Photos 5.1A through 5.1C as your instructor explains and demonstrates each performance cue for this skill.

Photo 5.1A
Forehand backwall stroke, backswing
(ball has come off back wall)

Photo 5.1B
Forehand back wall stroke, contact

Photo 5.1C
Forehand back wall
stroke, follow-through

PERFORMANCE CUES (Preparation)

1. **Grip:** Forehand grip.
2. **Court position** Out from the back wall, in the court area where you anticipate the ball to rebound from the back wall.
3. **Body position:** Nondominant side toward the front wall, chest to side wall.
4, **Backswing:** Abbreviated *loop*, and compact, to avoid hitting back wall.

PERFORMANCE CUES (Contact)

1. **Body weight transfer:** Forward from the rear foot to the front foot.
2. **Forward swing:** The racquet loops behind the body and starts forward toward the ball.
3. **Ball contact:** At or below the knees.

PERFORMANCE CUES (Follow-Through)

1. **Body rotation:** Hip and shoulders rotate to an open position.
2. **Forward swing:** Upward and across the body, and compact.
3. **Movement:** Move back to the center of the court immediately.

COMPREHENSION TASK

Find a partner and take turns. Execute the forehand back wall stroke at nearly full speed, *without hitting the ball*, until you feel comfortable with the stroke. Have your court partner use the **performance cues** to decide if your form is correct. Then switch roles and repeat this drill. Repeat this drill 3 times.

LEARNING TIPS

1. If the ball returning from the front wall has enough height and velocity to easily reach the back wall, do not "cut the ball off" and hit it before it reaches the back wall.
2. Avoid chasing the ball around the court and trying to play "catch-up." Read the walls and quickly move into the area of anticipated ball contact. Assume a hitting position and wait for the ball to come to you.
3. The higher and faster the ball rebounds from the front wall, the farther out it will rebound from the back wall. Set up accordingly.
4. The spin of the ball as it strikes the back wall will modify the rebound angle.
5. Allow the ball on the rebound from the back wall to travel just past your body before executing the shot.
6. Let the ball fall to the desired point of contact (at or below the knees) before stroking it.

READINESS DRILL

5-1.   Stand 3 to 5 feet from the back wall. With your non-racquet hand gently toss the ball 5 to 6 feet high on the back wall. (*Note*: It will take a few tries to get the toss correct.) Let the ball bounce once, and then return it to the front wall with a forehand stroke. Attempt to stroke the ball directly to the front wall. Repeat this drill 20 times.

If you experience difficulty with the readiness drill, refer to the **performance cues** and review each cue as presented. If you still have difficulty, ask your course instructor to assist you in applying these techniques.

Common Errors and Their Correction

Error	Correction
Ball drifts right into the side wall before contacting the front wall.	Adjust your point of ball contact forward toward the front wall.
Ball drifts across the center of the court.	Adjust your ball contact backwards towards the midline of your body.
Ball lacks velocity.	1. Transfer your body weight forward and into the point of ball contact. 2. Allow the ball to pass from the back wall to the front of your body before you contact it. 3. Rotate your wrist and forearm forward during the point of ball contact.

CRITERION TASK 5-1

Back Wall Forehand: Self-Checked

Stand 3 to 5 feet from the back wall and about 10 feet from the right side wall. Mark the spot with a cone or other marker (see Illustration 5.1). Gently toss the ball 5 to 6 feet high on the back wall. Let it bounce once, and then return it to the front wall with a forehand drive. To be counted as successful, a shot must travel directly from the racquet to the front wall without first striking the side wall, ceiling, or floor.

Practice this task in blocks of 10 shots. Record the number of successful shots for each block on the **Personal Recording Form**. When three block scores reach or exceed 7 out of 10, initial and date in the space provided.

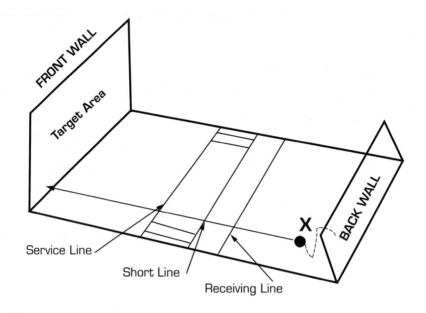

Illustration 5.1
Back wall forehand

Personal Recording Form									
Block 1	Block 2	Block 3	Block 4	Block 5	Block 6	Block 7	Block 8	Block 9	Block 10
___/10	___/10	___/10	___/10	___/10	___/10	___/10	___/10	___/10	___/10

Your initials _____   Date completed _____

BACKHAND BACK WALL STROKE

INSTRUCTOR DEMONSTRATION

Your course instructor will explain and demonstrate the key performance cues for the backhand back wall stroke. If you have questions, be sure to ask them before proceeding to the individualized task sequence. Refer to Photos 5.2A through 5.2C as your instructor explains and demonstrates each performance cue for this skill.

Photo 5.2A
Backhand back wall stroke, backswing (ball has come off back wall)

Photo 5.2B
Backhand back wall stroke, contact

Photo 5.2C
Backhand back wall stroke, follow-through

PERFORMANCE CUES (Preparation)

1. **Grip:** Backhand grip.
2. **Court position:** Out from the back wall. In the court area where you anticipate the ball to rebound from the back wall.
3. **Body position:** Dominant (racquet) side toward the front wall, chest to side wall.
4. **Backswing:** Abbreviated *loop*, and compact, to avoid hitting back wall.

PERFORMANCE CUES (Contact)

1. **Body weight transfer:** Forward from the rear foot to the front foot.
2. **Forward swing:** The racquet loops behind the body and starts forward toward the ball.
3. **Ball contact:** At or below the knees.

PERFORMANCE CUES (Follow-through)

1. **Body rotation:** Hip and shoulders rotate to an open position.
2. **Forward swing:** Upward and across the body, and compact.
3. **Movement:** Move back to the center of the court immediately.

COMPREHENSION TASK

Find a partner and take turns. Execute the backhand back wall stroke at nearly full speed, *without hitting the ball*, until you feel comfortable with the stroke. Have your court partner use the **performance cues** to decide if your form is correct. Then switch roles and repeat this drill. Repeat this drill 3 times.

LEARNING TIPS

1. If the ball returning from the front wall has enough height and velocity to easily reach the back wall, do not "cut the ball off" and hit it before it reaches the back wall.
2. Avoid chasing the ball around the court and trying to play "catch-up." Read the walls and quickly move into the area of anticipated ball contact. Assume a hitting position and wait for the ball to come to you.
3. The higher and faster the ball rebounds from the front wall, the farther out it will rebound from the back wall. Set up accordingly.
4. The spin of the ball as it strikes the back wall will modify the rebound angle.
5. Allow the ball on the rebound from the back wall to travel just past your body before executing the shot.
6. Let the ball fall to the desired point of contact (at or below the knees) before stroking it.

READINESS DRILL

5-1. Stand 3 to 5 feet from the back wall, dominant (racquet) side toward the front wall. Gently toss the ball with your nonracquet hand 5 to 6 feet high on the back wall. (*Note*: It will take a few tries to get the toss correct.) Let the ball bounce once, and then return it to the front wall with a backhand stroke. Attempt to stroke the ball directly to the front wall. Repeat this drill 20 times.

If you experiene difficulty with the readiness drill, please refer to the **performance cues** and review each cue as presented. If you still have difficulty, ask your course instructor to assist you in applying these techniques.

Common Errors and Their Correction

Error	Correction
Ball drifts left into the side wall before contacting the front wall.	Adjust your point of ball contact forward toward the front wall.
Ball drifts across the center of the court.	Adjust your ball contact backwards toward the mid-line of your body.
Ball lacks velocity.	1. Transfer your body weight forward and into the point of ball contact. 2. Allow the ball to pass from the back wall to the front of your body before you contact it. 3. Rotate your wrist and forearm forward during the point of ball contact.

CRITERION TASK 5-2

Back Wall Backhand: Self-Checked

Stand 3 to 5 feet from the back wall and about 10 feet from the side wall, nondominant (racquet) side toward the front wall. Mark the spot with a cone or other marker (see Illustration 5.2). Gently toss the ball 5 to 6 feet high on the back wall. Let it bounce once, and then return it to the front wall with a backhand drive. To be counted as successful, a shot must travel directly from the racquet to the front wall without first striking the side wall, ceiling, or floor.

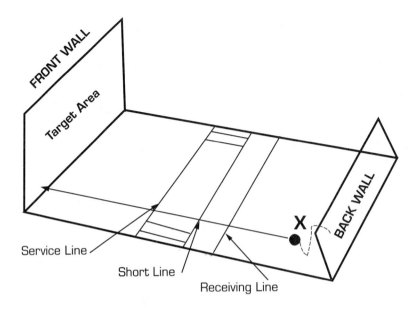

FRONT WALL

Target Area

BACK WALL

X

Service Line
Short Line
Receiving Line

Illustration 5.2
Back wall backhand

Practice this task in blocks of 10 shots. Record the number of successful shots for each block on the **Personal Recording Form**. When
three block scores reach or exceed 7 out of 10, initial and date in the
space provided.

Personal Recording Form									
Block 1	Block 2	Block 3	Block 4	Block 5	Block 6	Block 7	Block 8	Block 9	Block 10
___/10	___/10	___/10	___/10	___/10	___/10	___/10	___/10	___/10	___/10

Your initials _____ Date completed _____

CRITERION TASK 5-3

Back Wall Setup (Forehand and Backhand): Self-Checked

From the center of the court (X), stroke the ball to the front wall high enough and hard enough that it will bounce once and then rebound from the back wall (see Illustration 5.3). (*Note*: Practice the setup shot several times until you can execute it consistently.) Adjust your court position according to the rebound from the back wall so that you can stroke the ball to the front wall before it bounces a second time. To count as a successful shot, the ball must travel directly from the racquet to the front wall without first striking the side wall, ceiling, or floor.

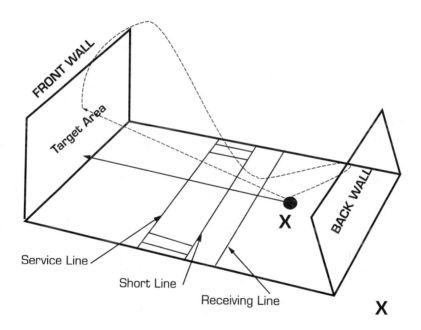

Illustration 5.3
Back wall setup

Practice from the forehand side first. Practice this task in blocks of 10 shots. Record the number of successful shots for each block on the **Personal Recording Form**. When three block scores reach or exceed 7 out of 10 on each side, initial and date in the spaces provided.

Forehand Side

Personal Recording Form									
Block 1	Block 2	Block 3	Block 4	Block 5	Block 6	Block 7	Block 8	Block 9	Block 10
___/10	___/10	___/10	___/10	___/10	___/10	___/10	___/10	___/10	___/10

Your initials _____ Date completed _____

Backhand Side

Personal Recording Form									
Block 1	Block 2	Block 3	Block 4	Block 5	Block 6	Block 7	Block 8	Block 9	Block 10
___/10	___/10	___/10	___/10	___/10	___/10	___/10	___/10	___/10	___/10

Your initials _____ Date completed _____

MODULE 6

CEILING SHOTS

INTRODUCTION

A ceiling shot hits the ceiling first (near the front wall), then hits high on the front wall, then hits the court and takes a big bounce, finally arcing very close to the back wall. It is most often a defensive shot, used to force the opponent out of the control zone so that you can occupy that area. This is called *neutralizing the point*. When hit with precision, the ceiling shot can be an offensive tactic, giving the opponent an extremely difficult shot to return and often resulting in a fault.

The shot can also be used to return serves. The ceiling shot can be executed with either a forehand (overhead) or backhand stroke. Practicing this shot will improve your racquetball skills and make you much more competitive. Many players consider this the shot that separates beginners from intermediates.

FOREHAND CEILING SHOT

INSTRUCTOR DEMONSTRATION

Your course instructor will explain and demonstrate the key performance cues for the forehand ceiling shot. If you have questions, be sure to ask them before proceeding to the individualized task sequence. Refer to Photos 6.1A through 6.1C as your instructor explains and demonstrates each performance cue for this skill.

Photo 6.1A
Forehand ceiling shot, backswing

Photo 6.1B
Forehand ceiling shot, contact

Photo 6.1C
Forehand ceiling shot, follow-through

PERFORMANCE CUES (Preparation)

1. **Grip:** Forehand grip.
2. **Backswing:** Take the racquet back into the *backscratch* position.
3. **Foot pivot:** Shift your body weight to your rear foot.
4. **Body rotation:** Hip and shoulders rotate clockwise.

PERFORMANCE CUES (Contact)

1. **Body weight transfer:** Take a short step forward with the lead foot. Body weight is shifted from the rear foot to the front foot.
2. **Ball contact:** Just forward of your body, overhead.
3. **Wrist:** Rotates with the forearm to provide power.

PERFORMANCE CUES (Follow-Through)

1. **Body rotation:** Hip and shoulders continue to rotate counterclockwise.
2. **Forward swing:** Forward, toward the front section of the ceiling.

COMPREHENSION TASK

Find a partner and take turns. Execute the forehand ceiling ball stroke, *without hitting the ball.* until you feel comfortable with the stroke. Have your court partner use the **Performance Cues** to decide if your forehand form is correct. Then switch roles and repeat this drill. Repeat this drill 3 times.

LEARNING TIPS

1. Be sure to get to the place at which the ball will drop "on your forehead" and set up in plenty of time.
2. Aim to hit the ceiling first, not the front wall. This is very important,
3. Hip and shoulder rotation turns the side of the body toward the front wall.
4. As you contact the ball, shift your body weight forward toward the front wall. Do not stand straight up
5. At the point of ball impact, rotate your wrist and forearm.
6. Follow-through is toward the front section of the ceiling.

READINESS DRILL

6-1. **Forehand ball-throwing drill.** Take the court position about 5 feet behind the receiving line in the center of the court. **Do not use your racquet for this drill.** Place a ball in your racquet hand and with a baseball-throwing motion throw the ball to the front section of the ceiling very near the front wall. This throwing motion is the same motion you use when executing a forehand ceiling ball. The flight of the ball should be in a straight line (parallel with the side wall) and the ball should contact the front part of the ceiling before striking the front wall. Repeat this drill 20 times. As you become more consistent, try throwing the ball harder.

If you experience difficulty with the readiness drill, refer to the **performance cues** and review each cue as presented. If you still have difficulty, ask your course instructor to assist you in applying these techniques.

Common Errors and Their Correction

Error	Correction
Ball hits the front wall before it contacts the ceiling.	Adjust your ball contact backward toward the mid-line of your body.
Ball hits the ceiling, but not high on the front wall.	Adjust your ball contact forward toward the front wall.
Ball lacks velocity.	1. Transfer your body weight forward into the point of ball contact.
	2. Swing harder!

CRITERION TASK 6-1

High Toss and Hit to Ceiling, Forehand: Self-Checked

Take the court position about 5 feet behind the receiving line in the center of the court. Toss the ball high into the air so that the ball will bounce well above your head. As the ball bounces from the floor, move under (but slightly to the rear) (X) the ball and hit a forehand ceiling ball to the front section of the ceiling. The ball flight should travel in a straight line (parallel with the side wall) to the front section of the ceiling before striking the front wall. To count as a successful shot, the ball must travel directly from the racquet to the ceiling, hit high on the front wall and take its first bounce past the receiving line *before* hitting the back wall. See Illustration 6.1.

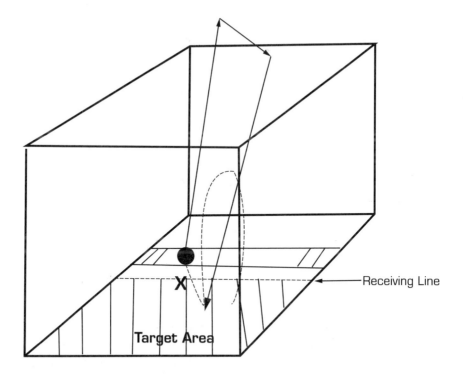

Illustration 6.1
High toss and hit (forehand ceiling ball)

Practice this task in blocks of 10 shots. Record the number of successful shots for each block on the Personal Recording Form. When three block scores reach or exceed 7 out of 10, initial and date in the space provided.

Personal Recording Form									
Block 1	Block 2	Block 3	Block 4	Block 5	Block 6	Block 7	Block 8	Block 9	Block 10
__/10	__/10	__/10	__/10	__/10	__/10	__/10	__/10	__/10	__/10

Your initials _____   Date completed _____

BACKHAND CEILING SHOT

INSTRUCTOR DEMONSTRATION

Your course instructor will explain and demonstrate the key performance cues for the backhand ceiling shot. If you have questions, be sure to ask them before proceeding to the individualized task sequence. Refer to Photos 6.2A through 6.2C as your instructor explains and demonstrates each performance cue for this skill.

PERFORMANCE CUES (Preparation)

1. **Grip:** Backhand grip.
2. **Backswing:** Take the racquet back toward the back wall.
3. **Foot pivot:** Shift your body weight to your rear foot.
4. **Body rotation:** Hip and shoulders rotate clockwise.

Photo 6.2A
Backhand ceiling shot, backswing

Photo 6.2B
Backhand ceiling shot, contact

Photo 6.2C
Backhand ceiling shot, follow-through

PERFORMANCE CUES (Contact)

1. **Body weight transfer:** Take a short step forward with the lead foot. Body weight is shifted from the rear foot to the front foot.
2. **Ball contact:** Just forward of your body.
3. **Wrist:** Rotates with the forearm to provide power.

PERFORMANCE CUES (Follow-through)

1. **Body rotation:** Hip and shoulders continue to rotate clockwise.
2. **Forward swing:** Forward, toward the front section of the ceiling.

COMPREHENSION TASK

Find a partner and take turns. Execute the backhand ceiling shot stroke *without a ball* until you feel comfortable with the stroke. Have your court partner use the **performance cues** to decide if your backhand form is correct. Then switch roles and repeat this drill. Repeat this drill 3 times.

READINESS DRILL

6-2.   Stand in the middle of the court about at the receiving line with your dominant (racquet) side toward the front wall. Make a high toss and let it hit the court. The toss should be high enough that it will bounce off the floor over your head on your backhand side. (*Note:* You may have to practice the toss several times before you become consistent, but do not hit errant tosses.) Hit controlled backhand ceiling shots that strike the ceiling first and then the front wall. Do not be concerned with a specific aiming point at this time. Work to develop a consistent pattern for this stroke. Do this drill until you have hit 30 backhand ceiling shots that strike the ceiling first and then the front wall (and no side walls).

If you experience difficulty with the readiness drill, refer to the **performance cues** and review each cue as presented. If you still have difficulty, ask your course instructor to assist you in applying these techniques.

Common Errors and Their Correction

Error	Correction
Ball hits the front wall before it contacts the ceiling.	Adjust your ball contact backward toward the mid-line of your body.
Ball hits the ceiling but not high on the front wall.	Adjust your ball contact forward toward the front wall.
Ball lacks velocity.	1. Transfer your body weight forward into the point of ball contact. 2. Swing harder!

CRITERION TASK 6-2

High Toss and Hit to Ceiling, Backhand: Self-Checked

Take the court position about 5 feet behind the receiving line on the left side of the court. Toss the ball high into the air so that the ball will bounce well above your head. As the ball bounces from the floor, move under (but slightly to the rear) (X) of the ball and hit a backhand ceiling ball to the front section of the ceiling. The ball flight should travel to the front section of the ceiling before striking the front wall. To count as a successful shot, the ball must travel directly from the racquet to the ceiling, hit high on the front wall, and take its first bounce past the receiving line *before* hitting the back wall. See Illustration 6.2.

Practice this task in blocks of 10 shots. Record the number of successful shots for each block on the Personal Recording Form. When three block scores reach or exceed 7 out of 10, initial and date in the space provided.

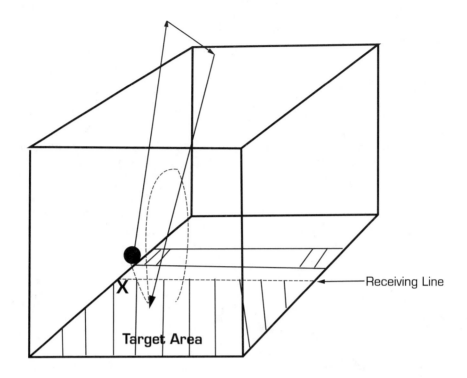

Illustration 6.2
High toss and hit (backhand ceiling ball)

Personal Recording Form									
Block 1	Block 2	Block 3	Block 4	Block 5	Block 6	Block 7	Block 8	Block 9	Block 10
___/10	___/10	___/10	___/10	___/10	___/10	___/10	___/10	___/10	___/10

Your initials _____   Date completed _____

CHALLENGE TASK

Partner Ceiling Ball Rally

Find a partner who has also completed Criterion Task 6-2. Make sure both players are wearing their eyeguards. Both players take positions in the back-court. One player initiates a partner rally drill by hitting a ceiling ball to the front wall. The other partner moves into position and plays a forehand or backhand shot in return. Both players attempt to keep the ball in play using only forehand and backhand ceiling shots. *The objective of this task is to keep the ball in play as long as possible using only ceiling shots.* Keep track of your longest rally and try to improve this score each time. You may repeat this task as often as you wish.

MODULE 7

SERVING

INTRODUCTION

Points can only be scored by the serving player or team (doubles), so the serve is an extremely important skill in racquetball. This is the only time that one player (the server) has the time and options to execute the shot of his or her choice, and force the opponent into a predictable return. Without a doubt, the serve starts the key strategic sequence in the point because the server holds a distinct advantage at this moment. Once this advantage is neutralized, it becomes "anyone's point" to win.

Because the server can determine the place on the court and the type of return to be made by the receiver, the server can further his or her advantage by moving into the key strategic spot immediately after striking the serve. After executing the serve, the server quickly relocates from the serving zone to the midcourt area, called the *control zone*. The control zone in racquetball is located just to the rear of the receiving line (see Illustration 7.1). When the server moves into this area of the court, he or she is in the optimal court position to hit a variety of offensive shots. To further this advantage, the server can *shade* his or her position within the control zone to the side nearest the receiver's return spot. Illustration 7.2 shows how to shade for serves to the receiver's backhand side. Illustration 7.3 shows how to shade for serves made to the receiver's forehand side.

FRONT WALL

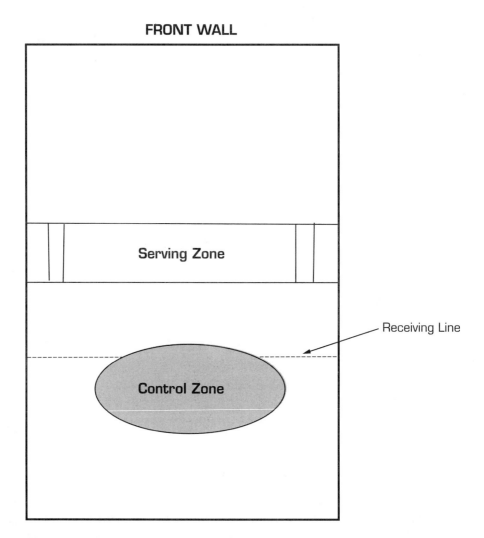

Illustration 7.1
Control zone

FRONT WALL

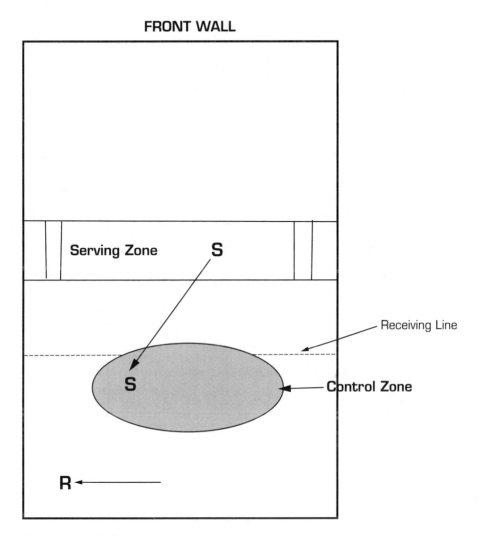

Illustration 7.2
Transition to the control position (serve to backhand
side of the court

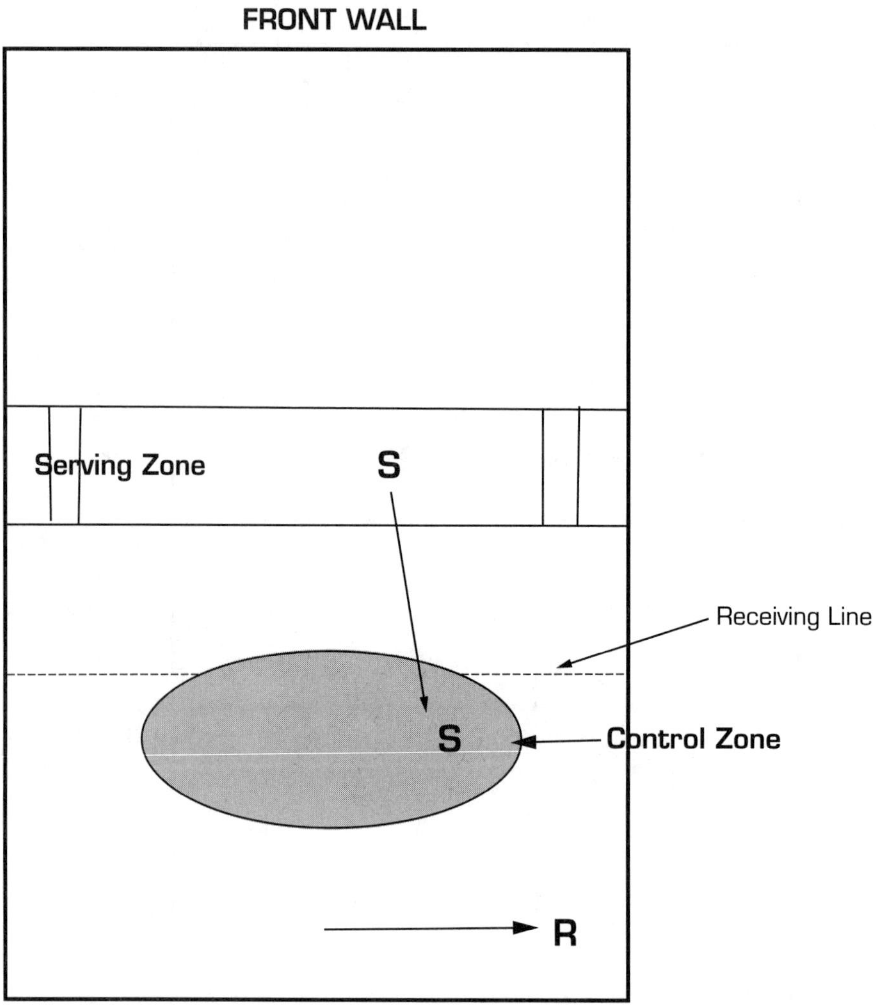

FRONT WALL

Serving Zone   S

S   Control Zone

Receiving Line

R

Illustration 7.3
Transition to the control position (serve to forehand
corner of the court)

BASIC SERVING RULES

In order to practice the tasks in this module correctly, you will need to be aware of some basic serving rules that apply in racquetball. Ask your instructor to demonstrate each rule briefly, and to give legal and nonlegal examples of each ruling.

1. The server must have both feet in the service zone when contact is made with the ball. A foot may be touching either the service line or short line, but may not be over these lines.
2. The racquet must strike the ball while the ball is in the service zone.
3. The server may not obstruct the receiver's view of the ball as the ball rebounds off the front wall (a *screen serve*).
4. The server may bounce and catch the ball prior to the serve attempt, but cannot do this to intentionally deceive the receiver.
5. Once the ball is released for the serve, it must bounce once on the court before being struck, but it cannot bounce more than once.
6. All serves must hit the front wall first (not to is a *nonfront serve*).
7. The serve must hit behind the short line on its first bounce on the floor. Hitting the line is "not good" (a *short serve*).
8. The serve cannot hit the ceiling (a *ceiling serve*).
9. The serve cannot hit more than two walls before bouncing to the floor (a *three-wall serve*).
10. The serve cannot hit the back wall before its first bounce on the floor (a *long serve*).

This is a lot of rules, but to practice correctly you must keep them in mind so that you will not develop bad habits in this module's task sequences. The three basic serves used in racquetball are the **drive serve**, the **Z-serve**, and the **lob serve**. Each serve has a different strategic purpose, and good players become proficient in all three types to vary the kinds of serves given to the opponent. Two basic strategies apply: (1) serve to the receiver's backhand side 90% of the time, and (2) whether hit to the backhand or forehand side, always force the receiver deep into one of the corners to make her or his return.

DRIVE SERVE

The drive serve is a high-velocity serve that travels low and hard from the front wall directly toward one of the rear corners of the court. It is the same technique as the forehand drive you learned in Module 3, hit very hard, close to the floor, and deep into the corner. Approximately 90% of all power serves are directed to the opponent's backhand corner.

INSTRUCTOR DEMONSTRATION

Your course instructor will explain and demonstrate the key performance cues for the drive serve. If you have questions, be sure to ask them before proceeding to the individualized task sequence. Refer to Photos 7.1A through 7.1C as your instructor explains and demonstrates each performance cue for this skill.

Photo 7.1A
Drive serve, setup and backswing

Photo 7.1B
Drive serve, contact

Photo 7.1C
Drive serve, follow-through

PERFORMANCE CUES (Preparation)

1. **Position:** Slightly right of center in service zone.
2. **Grip:** Forehand grip.
3. **Body position:** Inside the service area with your nondominant side toward the front wall.
4. **Ball presentation:** Drop the ball out to the side and forward of the lead foot.
5. **Aiming spot:** Three to four feet off the court, slightly to the left of center on the front wall.
6. **Target:** First bounce just past the short line and then deep into the receiver's backhand corner.

PERFORMANCE CUES (Contact)

1. **Body weight transfer:** Stride forward with the front foot.
2. **Forward swing:** The racquet loops behind the body and starts forward and downward toward the ball.
3. **Ball contact:** Just forward of the lead foot, below the knee.

PERFORMANCE CUES (Follow-through)

1. **Body rotation:** Hip and shoulders rotate toward the front wall.
2. **Forward swing:** Upward and across the body.
3. **Movement after serve:** To the control zone, shaded toward the receiver's backhand side.

COMPREHENSION TASK

Find a partner and take turns. Execute the drive serve stroke *without a ball* until you feel comfortable with the stroke. Have your court partner use the **performance cues** to decide if your form is correct. Then switch roles and repeat this drill. Repeat this drill 3 times.

LEARNING TIPS

1. The ball drop should be far enough in front and out to the side to allow for a full-swing power stroke.
2. Take a full stride into the stroke to allow for body weight transfer and hip and shoulder rotation.
3. Contact the ball low and hard enough to permit the rebound from the front wall to strike the court just to the rear of the short service line.
4. Watch for foot faults. *You are allowed to step on but not over the lines bounding the service area.*

5. The server should make a smooth transition from the serving zone into the control position on the court.

6. If the serve is directed to the backhand corner of the court, the server should shade to the left side of the control position. If the serve is directed to the forehand corner of the court, the server should shade to the right side of the control position.

7. Occasionally, a served ball will end up on the other side of the court from where it was supposed to go. If this occurs, the server must adjust his or her transition move to the appropriate side of the control area.

READINESS DRILLS

7-1. Take the correct position for the drive serve just to the right of center in the service zone. Drop the ball and stroke easy drive serves to the front wall. Use these attempts to find the spot on the front wall that will allow your serve to travel deep into the rear left corner of the court. This is your *vertical* aiming spot. Practice this drill until you have hit 30 drive serves that go into the rear-left corner, even if on more than one bounce. Do not be concerned with power at this time.

7-2. Take the correct position for the drive serve just to the right of center in the service zone. Drop the ball and stroke *hard* drive serves to the front wall. Use these attempts to find the spot up from the floor that will allow your serve to travel just over the short line and toward the rear left corner. This is your *horizontal* aiming spot. Practice this drill until you have hit 30 drive serves that go into the rear-left corner on no more than one bounce.

7-3. Take the correct position for the drive serve, just to the right of center in the service zone, and visualize the intersection of your vertical and horizontal aiming spots. (*Note: The aiming spot can vary a little for each person, depending on how hard each player can hit the drive serve;–the harder the serve, the lower the horizontal line will be.*) Hit hard drive serves, trying to hit close to your aiming target consistently. Do this drill until you have hit 30 accurate drive serves into the rear-left corner.

7-4. **Moving to the control zone.** Once you have completed Readiness Drill 7-3, hit 20 more drive serves to the backhand corner of the court. After the ball has passed the short serve line, quickly move into the control zone and set up for the next shot. Do not be concerned with serving accuracy on this drill. Work to move quickly into the proper part of the control position after each serve.

If you experience difficulty with the readiness drills, refer to the **performance cues** and review each cue as presented. If you still have difficulty, ask your course instructor to assist you in applying these techniques.

Common Errors and Their Correction

Error	Correction
Ball strikes the left side wall on the return from the front wall.	Adjust your serving target toward the middle of the front wall.
Serve travels down the middle of the court on the return from the front wall.	Adjust your serving target to the left on the front wall.
Serve lacks velocity.	1. Step forward with your front foot and transfer your body weight into the serve. 2. Rotate your hips and shoulders counter clockwise as you transfer your body weight into the serve. 3. Rotate your forearm and wrist during the point of contact.
Serve hits deep in the receiving court and rebounds too far out from the back wall.	Adjust your serving target downward (lower) on the front wall.

CRITERION TASK 7-1

Drive Serve to Backhand: Self-Checked

Place a small cone or other marker 6 feet from the left side wall and 6 feet from the back wall, forming a square in the rear left corner (see Illustration 7.4). Take a serving position just to the right of center in the service zone (X) and hit drive serves to the backhand side. To count as a successful serve, the serve must be legal in all ways, take its first bounce past the receiving line, and hit inside the target on the second bounce. *In addition, you must make the proper transition into the control zone on every attempt. Do not remain stationary between serve attempts.*

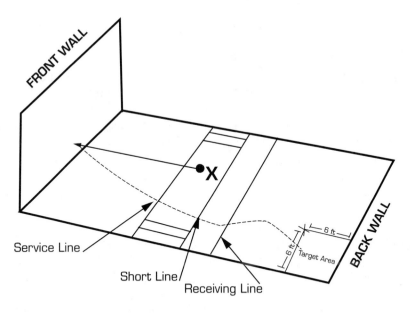

Illustration 7.4
Drive serve to backhand

Practice this task in blocks of 10 shots. Record the number of successful shots for each block on the **Personal Recording Form**. When three block scores reach or exceed 7 out of 10, initial and date in the space provided.

Personal Recording Form									
Block 1	Block 2	Block 3	Block 4	Block 5	Block 6	Block 7	Block 8	Block 9	Block 10
___/10	___/10	___/10	___/10	___/10	___/10	___/10	___/10	___/10	___/10

Your initials _____   Date completed _____

Z-SERVE

INTRODUCTION

The Z-serve is named from its flight pattern. This serve is usually hit from the left side of the serving area and is directed to the front wall near the right corner of the court. The ball strikes (1) the front wall near the corner, (2) side wall, (3) the floor, and then (4) the opposite side wall. **The ball must contact the court before hitting the second side wall.** This serve requires pinpoint accuracy. But, when it is hit accurately, it is very difficult to return, especially when hit to the backhand side of a beginning player.

INSTRUCTOR DEMONSTRATION

Your course instructor will explain and demonstre the key performance cues for the Z-serve to the backhand and forehand sides. If you have questions, be sure to ask them before proceeding to the individualized task sequence. You will note that the stroke is the same as that for the drive serve, so you can refer back to Photos 7.1A through 7.1C as your instructor explains and demonstrates each performance cue for this skill.

PERFORMANCE CUES (Preparation)

1. **Position:** Left side of service zone to serve to backhand. Slightly right of center in service zone to serve to forehand side.
2. **Grip:** Forehand grip.
3. **Body position:** Inside the service area with your nondominant side toward the front wall.
4. **Ball presentation:** Drop the ball out to the side and forward of the lead foot.
5. **Aiming spot:** About 4 to 6 feet off the court and about 2 feet from the side wall (remember, the serve must hit the front wall first).
6. **Target:** On fly to intended side past receiving line, close to the intended side wall (remember, the ball must hit the court before it hits the second side wall).

PERFORMANCE CUES (Contact)

1. **Body weight transfer:** Stride forward with the front foot.
2. **Forward swing:** The racquet loops behind the body and starts forward and downward toward the ball.
3. **Ball contact:** Just forward of the lead foot, at the knee.

PERFORMANCE CUES (Follow-through)

1. **Body rotation:** Hip and shoulders rotate toward the front wall.
2. **Forward swing:** Upward and across the body.
3. **Movement after serve:** To the control zone, shaded toward the *target* side.

COMPREHENSION TASK

Find a partner and take turns. Execute the set up and Z-serve stroke *without a ball* until you feel comfortable with the stroke. Have your court partner use the **performance cues** to decide if your form is correct. Then switch roles and repeat this drill. Repeat this drill 3 times.

LEARNING TIPS

1. The Z-serve hits the front wall first and then the side wall. The ball must then contact the court before striking the other side wall.
2. Allow the ball to enter the receiving court area before you exit the serving zone and move into the control position.
3. The front wall ball contact will determine the specific flight pattern of the serve. The closer the front wall contact point to the corners, the more severe the Z-pattern. This is called a *tight* Z-*serve.*
4. Watch for foot faults. *You are allowed to step on but not over the lines bounding the service area.*

READINESS DRILLS

7-5.   Take the correct position for the Z-serve to backhand on the left side of the service zone. Drop the ball and stroke *easy* Z-serves to the front wall. Use these attempts to find the spot on the front wall that will allow your serve to hit the front wall, then the side wall, and then travel into the rear-left corner of the court. This is your *vertical* aiming spot. Practice this drill until you have hit 30 Z-serves that go into the rear-left corner, even on more than one bounce. Do not be concerned with power at this time.

7-6.   Take the correct position for the Z-serve to backhand on the left side of the service zone. Drop the ball and stroke *hard* Z-serves to the front wall. Use these attempts to find the spot up from the floor that will allow your serve to travel well over the short line and toward the rear left corner. This is your *horizontal* aiming spot. Practice this drill until you have hit 30 Z-serves that go into the rear-left corner on no more than one bounce.

7-7. Take the correct position for the Z-serve to backhand, on the left side of the service zone, and visualize the intersection of your vertical and horizontal aiming spots. (*Note:* The aiming spot can vary a little for each person, depending on how hard each player can hit the drive serve; the harder the serve, the lower the horizontal line will be.) Hit hard Z-serves, trying to strike your aiming target consistently. Do this drill until you have hit 30 accurate Z-serves into the rear-left corner.

7-8. **Moving to the control zone.** Once you have completed Readiness Drill 7-7, hit 20 more Z-serves to the backhand corner of the court. After the ball has passed the short serve line, quickly move into the control zone and set up for the next shot. Do not be concerned with serving accuracy on this drill; work to move quickly into the proper part of the control position after each serve.

Now repeat Readiness Drills 7-5 through 7-8 for Z-serves to the *forehand side*. Your serving position will be to the right of center in the service zone, and your target will be the right-rear corner. (*Note:* Be careful to get out of the way of the serve as it comes off the first side wall; it will pass very near your setup position.)

If you are experiencing difficulty with the readiness drills, refer to the **performance cues** and review each cue as presented. If you still have difficulty ask your course instructor to assist you in applying these techniques,

Common Errors and Their Correction

Error	Correction
Ball strikes three walls (front and two sides) before contacting the court.	Adjust your contact point on the front wall more toward the center of the court (away from the corner).
Z-serve enters the center of the court, allowing the receiver to hit a drive shot in return.	Move your contact point on the front wall more toward the front wall–side wall junction.
Z-serve lacks power.	1. Adjust your contact point on the front wall higher (up from the floor).
Serve is consistently short.	2. Increase the velocity of the serve by stroking the ball harder. 3. Move aiming spot slightly higher on front wall.

CRITERION TASK 7-2

Z-serve to Backhand: Instructor-Checked

Mark off a rectangle that is 10 feet from the left side wall and 15 feet from the receiving line. Use a cone or other marker (see Illustration 7.5). Take a position to the left of center within the service area (X) and hit Z-serves to the backhand corner of the court. To be counted as successful, the serve must be legal in all ways, hit the front wall first, then the right side wall, and then continue across the court, taking its first court bounce in the defined target. *In addition, you must make the proper transition into the control zone on every attempt. Do not remain stationary between serve attempts.*

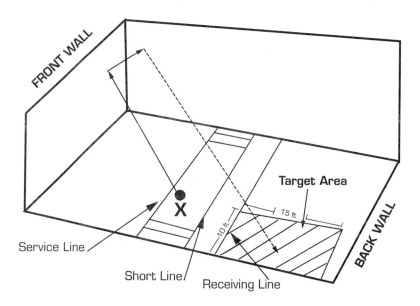

Illustration 7.5
Z-serve to backhand

Practice this task in blocks of 10 shots. Record the number of successful shots in each block on the **Personal Recording Form**. When your block scores consistently reach or exceed six, ask your instructor to observe and witness your attempt at criterion. Once your instructor has witnessed three successful blocks (6 of 10), have him or her initial and date in the space provided.

Personal Recording Form									
Block 1	Block 2	Block 3	Block 4	Block 5	Block 6	Block 7	Block 8	Block 9	Block 10
___/10	___/10	___/10	___/10	___/10	___/10	___/10	___/10	___/10	___/10

Instructor's initials _____ Date completed _____

CRITERION TASK 7-3

Z-serve to Forehand: Self-checked

Mark off a rectangle that is 10 feet from the right side wall and 15 feet from the receiving line. Use a cone or other marker (see Illustration 7.6). Take a position just to the right of center in the service area (X) and hit Z-serves to the forehand corner of the court. To be counted as successful, the serve must be legal in all ways, hit the front wall first, then the left side wall, and then continue across the court, taking its first court bounce in the defined target. *In addition, you must make the proper transition into the control zone on every attempt. Do not remain stationary between serve attempts.*

Practice this task in blocks of 10 shots. Record the number of successful shots for each block on the **Personal Recording Form**. When three block scores reach or exceed 6 out of 10, initial and date in the space provided.

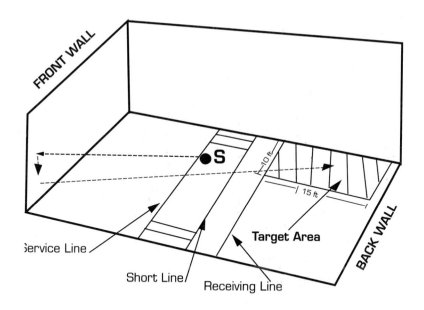

Illustration 7.6
Z-serve to forehand

Personal Recording Form									
Block 1	Block 2	Block 3	Block 4	Block 5	Block 6	Block 7	Block 8	Block 9	Block 10
___/10	___/10	___/10	___/10	___/10	___/10	___/10	___/10	___/10	___/10

Your initials _____   Date completed _____

LOB SERVE

INTRODUCTION

The lob serve is the most underrated serve in the game of racquetball, perhaps because it lacks the velocity of the drive and Z-serves, and appears "innocent." However, when hit accurately, it can be very effective. It is also relatively easy to learn. When executed correctly, the lob serve forces the receiver to contact the ball above the waist, most often forcing a defensive return. The lob serve is hit very softly and high on the front wall, as close as possible to the ceiling but not touching the ceiling. This produces a high, arcing bounce into the back corner, making for a difficult return by the receiver.

INSTRUCTOR DEMONSTRATION

Your course instructor will explain and demonstrate the key performance cues for the lob serve to the backhand and forehand sides. If you have questions, be sure to ask them before proceeding to the individualized task sequence. Refer to Photos 7.2A through 7.2C as your instructor explains and demonstrates each performance cue for this skill.

Photo 7.2A
Lob serve, setup and backswing

Photo 7.2B
Lob serve, contact

Photo 7.2C
Lob serve, follow-through

PERFORMANCE CUES (Preparation)

1. **Position:** Slightly right of center in the service zone to lob to backhand. Well left of center in service zone to lob to forehand side.
2. **Grip:** Forehand grip.
3. **Body position:** Inside the service area with your nondominant side toward the front wall.
4. **Ball presentation:** Drop the ball out to the side and forward of the lead foot.
5. **Aiming spot:** Midway or higher up the front wall and slightly toward the target side (remember, the serve must hit the front wall first and cannot hit the ceiling).
6. **Target:** On high fly to intended side, close to the intended side and back walls (remember, the ball must hit the court before it hits a second wall).

PERFORMANCE CUES (Contact)

1. **Body weight transfer:** Stride forward with the front foot.
2. **Forward swing:** The racquet softly loops behind the body and starts forward with a lifting motion.
3. **Racquet face:** Tilted upward to help lift the ball.
4. **Ball contact:** Just forward of the lead foot, at the knee.

PERFORMANCE CUES (Follow-Through)

1. **Body rotation:** Hip and shoulders rotate toward the front wall.
2. **Forward swing:** Upward and across the body.
3. **Movement after serve:** To the control zone, shaded toward the *target* side.

COMPREHENSION TASK

Find a partner and take turns. Execute the setup and lob serve stroke *without a ball* until you feel comfortable with the stroke. Have your court partner use the **performance cues** to decide if your form is correct. Then switch roles and repeat this drill. Repeat this drill 3 times.

LEARNING TIPS

1. Drop the ball from about waist height to assure that the rebound from the court will allow you to get your racquet under the ball.

2. Contact the ball with the face of the racquet tilted backward (open face).
3. **Gently lift the ball** with the racquet toward the front wall.
4. The ball should travel on a high arc, very near the ceiling.
5. The ball should take a high bounce from the court and gently fall into the proper rear corner of the court.

READINESS DRILLS

7-9. Take the correct position for the lob serve to backhand on the right side of the service zone. Drop the ball and stroke lob serves to the front wall. Use these attempts to find the spot on the front wall that will allow your serve to hit the front wall and travel into the rear left corner of the court. This is your *vertical* aiming spot. Practice this drill until you have hit 30 lob serves that go into the rear-left corner, even if they are long or short.

7-10. Take the correct position for the lob serve to backhand on the right side of the service zone. Drop the ball and stroke lob serves to the front wall. Use these attempts to find the spot up from the floor that will allow your serve to travel on a high arc toward the rear left corner. This is your horizontal aiming spot. Practice this drill until you have hit 30 lob serves that go near the ceiling and deep into the rear-left corner.

7-11. Take the correct position for the lob serve to backhand on the right side of the service zone, and visualize the intersection of your vertical and horizontal aiming spots. (*Note:* the aiming spot can vary a little for each person, depending on how much lift each player can generate; the more lift, the lower on the wall you can aim.) Hit 30 legal and accurate lob serves, trying to hit close your aiming target consistently.

7-12. **Moving to the control zone.** Once you have completed Readiness Drill 7-11, hit 20 more lob serves to the backhand corner of the court. After the ball has passed the short serve line, quickly move into the control position and set up for the next shot. Do not be concerned with serving accuracy on this drill; work to move quickly into the proper part of the control zone after each serve.

Now repeat Readiness Drills 7-9 through 7-12 for lob serves to the *forehand side*. **Your serving position will be well left of center in the service zone, and your target will be the right-rear corner.**

If you experience difficulty with the readiness drills, refer to the **performance cues** and review each cue as presented. If you still have difficulty, ask your course instructor to assist you in applying these techniques.

Common Errors and Their Correction

Error	Correction
The serve contacts the side wall and drifts into the middle of the receiving area of the court.	Adjust your vertical aiming line more toward the center of the front wall.
The serve comes off the front wall too low and sets up for an offensive return of serve.	1. Adjust your horizontal aiming line upward **and** 2. Reduce the force of your stroke by **gently** stroking (lifting) the ball upward to the target area on the front wall.
The serve is too long.	Strike the ball easier, with more lift.

CRITERION TASK 7-4

Lob Serve to Backhand: Instructor-Checked

Mark off a square that is 8 feet from the left side wall and 8 feet from the back wall. Use a cone or other marker at that intersection (see Illustration 7.7). Take a position to the right of center within the service area (X) and hit lob serves to the backhand corner of the court. To be counted as successful, the serve must be legal in all ways, hit the front wall first, and pass near the ceiling, taking its first court bounce in the defined target. *In addition, you must make the proper transition into the control zone on every attempt. Do not remain stationary between serve attempts.*

Practice this task in blocks of 10 shots. Record the number of successful shots in each block on the **Personal Recording Form**. When your block scores consistently reach or exceed seven, ask your instructor to observe and witness your attempt at criterion. Once your instructor has witnessed three successful blocks (7 of 10), have him or her initial and date in the space provided.

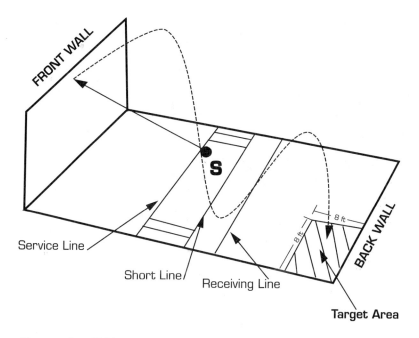

Illustration 7.7
Lob serve to backhand

Personal Recording Form									
Block 1	Block 2	Block 3	Block 4	Block 5	Block 6	Block 7	Block 8	Block 9	Block 10
__/10	__/10	__/10	__/10	__/10	__/10	__/10	__/10	__/10	__/10

Instructor's initials _____   Date completed _____

CRITERION TASK 7-5

Lob Serve to Forehand: Self-Checked

Mark off a square that is 8 feet from the right side wall and 8 feet from the back wall. Use a cone or other marker at that intersection (see Illustration 7.8). Take a position well left in the service area (X) and hit lob serves to the forehand corner of the court. To be counted as successful, the serve must be legal in all ways, hit the front wall first, and pass near the ceiling, taking its first court bounce in the defined target. *In addition, you must make the proper transition into the control zone on every attempt. Do not remain stationary between serve attempts.*

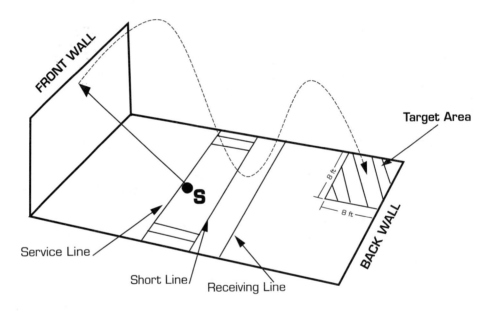

Illustration 7.8
Lob serve to forehand

Practice this task in blocks of 10 shots. Record the number of successful shots for each block on the **Personal Recording Form**. When three block scores reach or exceed 6 out of 10, initial and date in the space provided.

Personal Recording Form									
Block 1	Block 2	Block 3	Block 4	Block 5	Block 6	Block 7	Block 8	Block 9	Block 10
__/10	__/10	__/10	__/10	__/10	__/10	__/10	__/10	__/10	__/10

Your initials _____ Date completed _____

CHALLENGE TASK

Lob Serves

Find one or more students who have also completed Criterion Task 7-5. Place a large cardboard box, about the size of one used to ship a computer or medium-sized television, snugly in the backhand corner of the court. Tuck the box flaps in, or cut them off. Take a position just to the right of the center of the court within the service area and hit a lob serve. Each player will hit 10 serves in rotation. On the rebound from the front wall, the ball should first strike the court area just to the rear of the short service line, take a high bounce, and fall gently into the cardboard box. The scoring is as follows:

Illegal serve or not hitting the box *on the fly*	0 points
Hitting an outer side of the box *on the fly*	1 point
Hitting inside the box and bouncing out	2 points
Hitting and staying inside the box	3 points

The player with the highest point total after 10 rounds is the winner. Play several games to the backhand side and then several games to the forehand side.

MODULE **8**

RETURNING SERVES

INTRODUCTION

Since the server holds a temporary advantage when each point begins, it is essential that all players develop the skills needed to return serves effectively. Effectiveness comes in three degrees. At the very least the receiver must return the serve with a nonfault shot; otherwise the point is won immediately by the server. Next, the returner should hit a defensive return that will not allow the server to make an offensive shot on his or her next shot; this is called *neutralizing* the serve. Finally, on those few occasions when the server makes an errant serve, the receiver should be ready to counter right away with an offensive shot of his or her own, trying for a sideout off the serve.

The base position for returning serves is in the middle of the court (left to right), about two steps in front of the back wall. Assume a good ready position as the server prepares to make the serve. You might choose to "cheat" to the backhand side, **no more than a half step**, anticipating that most serves will come to that side. At the same time you will need to be prepared for Z-serves and the rare drive serve that will come to your forehand side.

RULES FOR RETURNING SERVES

You will learn the complete rules for racquetball in Module 10. But to practice the tasks in this module correctly, you will need to be aware of some basic rules that apply to returning serves in racquetball. Ask your instructor to demonstrate each of these rules briefly and to give legal and nonlegal examples of each ruling.

1. The receiver must be behind the receiving line when the serve is made.
2. The receiver cannot step over the short service line to make a return. She or he can step on the line, but not fully over it.

3. A serve that hits the back wall/floor crotch is considered "good" and is in play.
4. A serve that hits the crotch of a **second** wall and the floor is "not good."
5. If the receiver's view of the ball is obstructed unintentionally by the server, the receiver declares "screen serve" and the serve is taken over.
6. The return can be made by hitting any wall(s) before hitting the front wall, before the first bounce on the floor. This means you can project the ball off the back wall to the front wall, if needed.
7. Any return that hits the floor before the front wall is a point for the server; a shot that hits the front wall floor crotch is "not good" and results in a point for the server.

RETURNING THE DRIVE SERVE TO BACKHAND

As you learned in Module 7, the drive serve to the backhand side is fast, powerful, and low. Its purpose is to force an error immediately; therefore, the receiver must be ready at all times for this serve and move quickly into position in the backhand corner. The best defense for a power serve is an equally strong return of service. The key is for the player to focus on an **aggressive** backhand return of serve that takes the court advantage from the server. The most often selected offensive returns are the **up-the-wall kill shot** and the **V-pass cross court shot**. If the drive serve is difficult to handle, a **ceiling shot** is recommended as a defensive tactic.

UP-THE-WALL KILL SHOT

A kill shot is any shot hit low and hard to the front wall so that it rebounds quickly and out of reach of the opponent. It is hit with the same technique as for the backhand drive, with the contact point well below the knee. The objective is to hit this shot close to and parallel with the side wall so that it bounces straight back off the front wall and into the deep backhand corner, out of reach of the server.

INSTRUCTOR DEMONSTRATION

Your course instructor will explain and demonstrate the key performance cues for the up-the-wall kill shot from a backhand drive serve. If you have questions, be sure to ask them before proceeding to the individualized task sequence. Refer to Illustration 8.1 as your instructor explains and demonstrates each performance cue for this skill.

COMPREHENSION TASK

On the court with a partner, assume the ready position for returning a serve. Have your partner say "go," with no prior warnings. On "go," move to the left side wall, set yourself, and make the stroke for an up-the-wall skill shot *without hitting the ball*. Your partner should observe your technique and evaluate it the same way as for a backhand drive shot, pointing out correct and incorrect parts of your technique. Do this drill 10 times and then switch roles with your partner.

READINESS DRILL

8-1.　Find a partner and make sure both of you are wearing eyeguards. You will stand in the proper position for receiving serves (R). Your partner (S) serves a low, medium-paced drive serve to your backhand side and moves to the middle of the control zone (refer back to Illustration 8.1).

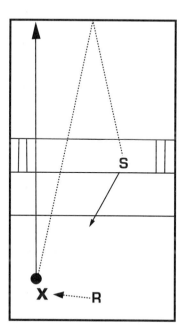

Move into position (X) and return this serve with an up-the-wall kill shot, aiming for the left half of the front wall. The ball should rebound so that it comes back between the left wall and your partner. **The serving partner should not attempt to hit your return shot; he or she should just stand in the control zone to help determine your target "alley."** Practice this drill until you have hit 20 successful shots. Switch roles with your partner after every five attempts.

If you experience difficulty with the readiness drill, refer to the **performance cues** and review each cue as presented. If you still have difficulty, ask your course instructor to assist you in applying these techniques.

Illustration 8.1
Up-the-wall kill shot from a drive serve

V-PASS CROSS-COURT

The V-pass cross-court return can be used when the server is positioned to the left side of the control zone, most likely in anticipation of an up-the-wall kill shot return. This leaves the right side of the court open for your return. This shot can also be used when the drive serve bounces too high to attempt a kill shot. It is hit with the same technique as the backhand drive, with the contact point about waist-high. The objective is to hit this shot close to the middle of the front wall so that it bounces deep into the forehand corner, out of reach of the server.

INSTRUCTOR DEMONSTRATION

Your course instructor will explain and demonstrate the key performance cues for the V-pass cross-court shot from a backhand drive serve. If you have questions, be sure to ask them before proceeding to the individualized task sequence. Refer to Illustration 8.2 as your instructor explains and demonstrates the performance cue for this skill

COMPREHENSION TASK

On the court with a partner, assume the ready position for returning a serve. Have your partner say "go," with no prior warning. On "go," move to the left side wall, set yourself, and make the stroke for the V-pass cross-court shot without *hitting the ball*. Your partner should observe your technique and evaluate it the same way as for a backhand drive shot, pointing out correct and incorrect parts of your technique. Do this drill 10 times and then switch roles with your partner.

READINESS DRILL

8-2. Find a partner and make sure both of you are wearing eyeguards. You will stand in the proper position for receiving serves (R). Your partner (S) serves a medium-paced drive serve to your backhand side (about waist-high for you) and moves to the middle of the control zone (refer to Illustration 8.2). Move into position (X) and return this serve with a V-pass cross-court shot, aiming for the middle of the front wall. The ball should rebound so that it comes back between the right wall and your partner. **The serving partner should not attempt to hit your return shot; he or she should just stand in the control zone to help determine your target "alley."** Practice this drill until

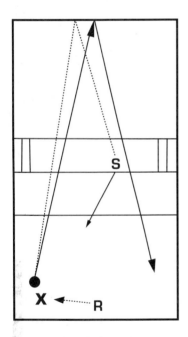

Illustration 8.2
V-pass cross-court from a drive serve

you have hit 20 successful shots. Switch roles with your partner after every five attempts.

If you are experience difficulty with the readiness drill, refer to the **performance cues** and review each cue as presented. If you still have difficulty, ask your course instructor to assist you in applying these techniques.

CEILING SHOT RETURN

The backhand ceiling shot return can be used when the server has hit a drive serve that bounces off the back wall high, well above your waist. It is hit with the same technique as for the backhand ceiling shot you learned earlier, with the contact point about head-high. The objective is to hit this shot to either corner, moving the server well out of the control zone. Once vacated, you can take over the control zone.

INSTRUCTOR DEMONSTRATION

Your course instructor wil explain and demonstrate the key performance cues for the ceiling shot return from a backhand drive serve. If you have questions, be sure to ask them before proceeding to the individualized task sequence. Refer to Illustration 8.3 as your instructor explains and demonstrates each performance cue for this skill

COMPREHENSION TASK

On the court with a partner, assume the ready position for returning a serve. Have your partner say "go," with no prior warnings. On "go," move to the left side wall, set yourself, and make the stroke for the ceiling shot return

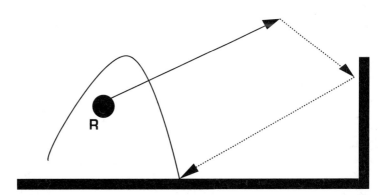

Illustration 8.3
Ceiling shot (side view)
from a drive serve

without *hitting the ball*. Your partner should observe your technique and evaluate it the same way as a for backhand drive shot, pointing out correct and incorrect parts of your technique. Do this drill 10 times and then switch roles with your partner.

READINESS DRILL

8-3. Find a partner and make sure both of you are wearing eyeguards. You will stand in the proper position for receiving serves (R). Your partner (serves a medium-paced drive serve to your backhand side (about head-high for you) and moves to the middle of the control zone (refer to Illustration 8.3). Move into position and return this serve with a ceiling shot. The ball should rebound so that it forces the server to move deep into one of the corners. **The serving partner should not attempt to hit your return shot; he or she should move into the control zone, and then track the ball into the corner.** Practice this drill until you have hit 20 successful shots. Switch roles with your partner after every five attempts.

If you experience difficulty with the readiness drill, refer to the **performance cues** and review each cue as presented. If you still have difficulty, ask your course instructor to assist you in applying these techniques.

LEARNING TIPS

1. Focus on the server until the serving motion begins, then shift your focus to the ball.
2. Don't make automatic assumptions as to where the ball will be served. Premature movement can place you at a disadvantage.
3. Attempt to hit an aggressive service return that will take the court advantage from the server.
4. If the serve is a *setup* (an errant serve), attempt to hit an up-the-wall kill shot return.
5. An effective service return will force the server from the control position of center court.
6. A ceiling return is recommended when the serve is difficult to return.

Common Errors and Their Correction

Error	Correction
Return of serve lacks power.	Move quickly to anticipate ball contact. Set up for the stroke to avoid hitting "on the run."
Return of serve provides the server with an easy kill shot.	Be aggressive. Hit a hard up-the-wall return (kill shot if possible).

RETURNING THE Z-SERVE

As you will recall, the Z-serve is used to force the receiver to the backhand side, near the left side wall. Its tricky bounce pattern is intended to fool the receiver into setting up incorrectly and hitting a weak shot in return. For beginners, the return of a well-placed Z-serve is often a fault. The choice of shot with which to return a Z-serve usually depends on the quality of the serve. If the Z-serve is weak or poorly placed, an **up-the-wall kill shot** can be attempted. If the Z-serve is not difficult to handle or bounces to you at about waist level, then a **V-pass** return would be a good choice. If the Z-serve is too difficult to handle with an offensive return, the recommended return is the **ceiling shot**. This return is the safest, and if it is well hit, this stroke will often generate a weak response from your opponent.

UP-THE-WALL KILL SHOT

The up-the-wall kill shot off a Z-serve is hit with the same technique as for the backhand drive, with the contact point well below the knee. The objective is to hit this shot close to and parallel with the side wall so that it bounces straight back off the front wall and into the deep back-hand corner, out of reach of the server.

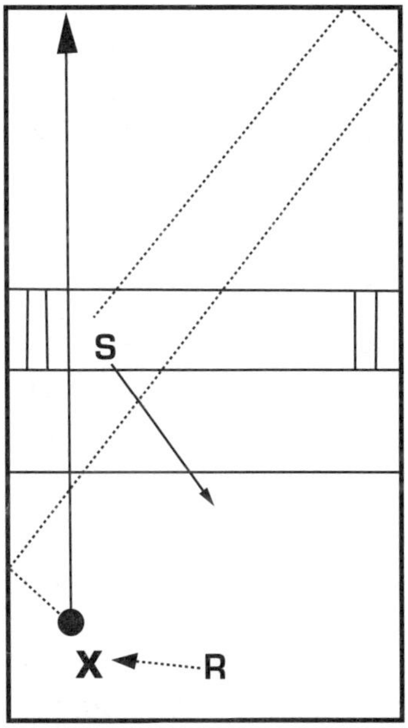

INSTRUCTOR DEMONSTRATION

Your course instructor will explain and demonstrate the key performance cues for the up-the-wall kill shot from a Z-serve to the backhand side. If you have questions, be sure to ask them before proceeding to the individualized task sequence. Refer to Illustration 8.4 as your instructor explains and demonstrates each performance cue for this skill

READINESS DRILL

8-4. Find a partner and make sure both of you are wearing eyeguards. You will stand in the proper position for receiving serves (R). Your partner (S) serves a medium-paced Z-serve to your backhand side and moves to the middle of the control zone (refer to Illustration 8.4). Move into position (X) and return this serve with an up-the-wall kill shot, aiming for the far left side of the front wall. The ball should rebound so that it comes back between the left wall and your partner. The serving partner should not attempt to hit your

Illustration 8.4
Up-the-wall kill shot from a Z-serve

return shot; he or she should just stand in the control zone to help determine your target "alley." Practice this drill until you have hit 20 successful shots. Switch roles with your partner after every five attempts.

If you experience difficulty with the readiness drill, refer to the **performance cues** and review each cue as presented. If you are still having difficulty, ask your course instructor to assist you in applying these techniques.

V-PASS CROSS-COURT

The V-pass cross-court return of a Z-serve to the backhand side can be used when the server is positioned to the left side of the control zone, most likely in anticipation of an up-the-wall kill shot return. This leaves the right side of the court open for your return. This shot can also be used when the Z-serve bounces too high to attempt a kill shot. It is hit with the same technique as the backhand drive, with the contact point about waist-high. The objective is to hit this shot close to the middle of the front wall so that it bounces deep into the forehand corner, out of reach of the server.

INSTRUCTOR DEMONSTRATION

Your course instructor will explain and demonstrate the key performance cues for the V-pass cross-court shot from a Z-serve to the backhand side. If you have questions, be sure to ask them before proceeding to the individualized task sequence. Refer to Illustration 8.5 as your instructor explains and demonstrates each performance cue for this skill

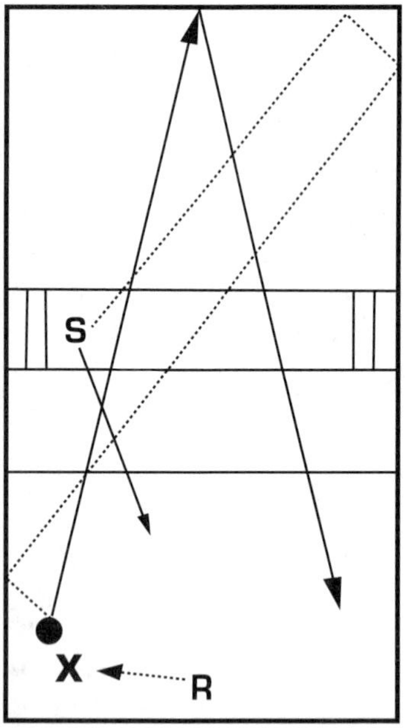

READINESS DRILL

8-5. Find a partner and make sure both of you are wearing eyeguards. You will stand in the proper position for receiving serves (R). Your partner (S) serves a medium-paced Z-serve to your backhand side (about waist-high for you) and moves to the middle of the control zone (refer to Illustration 8.5). Move into position (X) and return this serve with a V-pass cross-court shot, aiming for the middle of the front wall. The ball should rebound so that it comes back between the right wall and your partner. **The serving partner should not attempt to hit your return shot; he or she should just stand in the control zone to help determine your tar-**

Illustration 8.5
V-pass cross-court from a Z-serve

get **"alley."** Practice this drill until you have hit 20 successful shots. Switch roles with your partner after every five attempts.

If you experience difficulty with the readiness drill, refer to the **performance cues** and review each cue as presented. If you still have difficulty, ask your course instructor to assist you in applying these techniques.

CEILING SHOT RETURN

The backhand ceiling shot return can be used when the Z-serve to the backhand side bounces off the back wall high, well above your waist. It is hit with the same technique as for the backhand ceiling shot you learned earlier, with the contact point about head-high. The objective is to hit this shot to either corner, moving the server well out of the control zone. Once vacated, you can take over the control zone.

INSTRUCTOR DEMONSTRATION

Your course instructor will explain and demonstrate he key performance cues for the ceiling shot return from a Z-serve to the backhand side. If you have questions, be sure to ask them before proceeding to the individualized task sequence. Refer to Illustration 8.6 as your instructor explains and demonstrates each performance cue for this skill

READINESS DRILL

8-6.   Find a partner and make sure both of you are wearing eyeguards. You will stand in the proper position for receiving serves (R). Your partner serves a medium-paced drive Z-serve to your backhand side (about head-high for you) and moves to the middle of the control zone (refer to Illustration 8.6). Move into position and return this serve with a ceiling shot. The ball should rebound so that it forces the server to move deep into one of the corners. **The serving partner should not attempt**

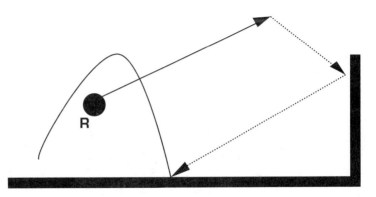

Illustration 8.6
Ceiling shot (side view)
from a Z-serve

to hit your return shot; he or she should move into the control zone, and then track the ball into the corner. Practice this drill until you have hit 20 successful shots. Switch roles with your partner after every five attempts.

If you experience difficulty with the readiness drill, refer to the **performance cues** and review each cue as presented. If you still have difficulty, ask your course instructor to assist you in applying these techniques.

LEARNING TIPS

1. On occasion, attempt to return the Z-serve before it reaches the second wall. This is termed *"cutting off the Z-serve"* and will often deny the server the required time to relocate to the control position.
2. Use a variety of returns. Generally, if the serve generates a *setup* (an errant serve), then a kill shot or V-pass is recommended.
3. If you are forced to contact the ball above your waist, a ceiling shot is the recommended return.
4. Don't underestimate the value of a ceiling shot return of serve. A well executed ceiling shot will force the server from the control position and allow you ample time to relocate your court position into that area.

Common Errors and Their Correction

Error	Correction
Return of serve lacks power.	Improved footwork and reading the walls will allow you to set up for the return of serve.
Return of serve provides the server with an easy kill shot.	1. Use a variety of service returns. 2. Be aggressive when the serve does not pressure you.

RETURNING THE LOB SERVE TO BACKHAND

As you will recall, the lob serve is hit high off the front wall, travels near the ceiling, and lands deep in the backhand corner. When placed accurately, it is a deceivingly difficult serve to return. When it is not accurate, it provides the returner with a good opportunity to make an offensive shot, even winning the hand-out immediately. Because many beginning players do not have the power for effective drive and Z-serves, they rely on the lob serve more than experienced players, making it important that you can return this serve as this stage of your development.

The choice of shot with which to return a lob serve usually depends on the quality of the serve. If the lob serve is weak or poorly placed, an **up-the-wall kill shot** can be attempted. If the lob serve is not difficult to handle or bounces to you at about waist level, then a **V-pass** return would be a good choice. If the lob serve is too difficult to handle with an offensive return or bounces to you at about head-high, the recommended return is the **ceiling shot**. This return is the safest and, if it is well hit, often generates a weak response from your opponent.

UP-THE-WALL KILL SHOT

The up-the-wall kill shot off a lob serve is hit with the same technique as for the backhand drive, with the contact point well below the knee. The objective is to hit this shot close to and parallel with the side wall so that it bounces straight back off the front wall and into the deep backhand corner, out of reach of the server.

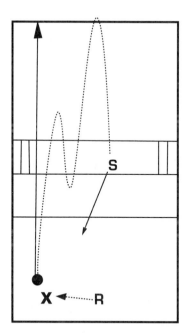

Illustration 8.7
Up-the-wall kill shot from a lob serve

INSTRUCTOR DEMONSTRATION

Your course instructor will explain and demonstrate the key performance cues for the up-the-wall kill shot from a lob serve to the backhand side. If you have questions, be sure to ask them before proceeding to the individualized task sequence. Refer to Illustration 8.7 as your instructor explains and demonstrates each performance cue for this skill

READINESS DRILL

8-7.   Find a partner and make sure both of you are wearing eyeguards. You will stand in the proper position for receiving serves (R). Your partner (S) makes a lob serve to your backhand side and moves to the middle of the control zone (refer to Illustration 8.7). Move into position (X) and return this serve with an up-the-wall kill shot, aiming for the left half of the front wall. The ball should rebound so that it comes back between the left wall and your partner. **The serving partner should not attempt to hit your return shot; he or she should just stand in the control zone to help determine your target "alley."** Practice this drill until you have hit 20 successful shots. Switch roles with your partner after every five attempts.

If you experience difficulty with the readiness drill, efer to the **performance cues** and review each cue as presented. If you still have difficulty, ask your course instructor to assist you in applying these techniques.

V-PASS CROSS-COURT

The V-pass cross-court return of a lob serve to the backhand side can be used when the server is positioned to the left side of the control zone, most likely in anticipation of an up-the-wall kill shot return. This leaves the right side of the court open for your return. This shot can also be used when the lob serve bounces too high to attempt a kill shot. It is hit with the same technique as the backhand drive, with the contact point about waist-high. The objective is to hit this shot close to the middle of the front wall so that it bounces deep into the forehand corner, out of reach of the server.

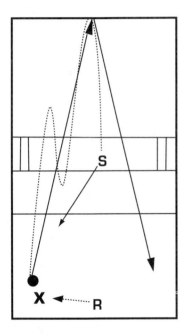

Illustration 8.8
V-pass cross-court from a lob serve

INSTRUCTOR DEMONSTRATION

Your course instructor will explain and demonstrate the key performance cues for the V-pass cross-court shot from a lob serve to the backhand side. If you have questions, be sure to ask them before proceeding to the individualized task sequence. Refer to Illustration 8.8 as your instructor explains and demonstrates each performance cue for this skill

READINESS DRILL

8-8. Find a partner and make sure both of you are wearing eyeguards. You will stand in the proper position for receiving serves (R). Your partner (S) makes a lob serve to your backhand side (about waist-high for you) and moves to the middle of the control zone (Refer to Illustration 8.8). Move into position and return this serve with a V-pass cross-court shot, aiming for the middle of the front wall. The ball should rebound so that it comes back between the right wall and your partner. **The serving partner should not attempt to hit your return shot; he or she should just stand in the control zone to help determine your target "alley."** Practice this drill until you have hit 20 successful shots. Switch roles with your partner after every five attempts.

If you experience difficulty with the readiness drill, refer to the **performance cues** and review each cue as presented. If you still have difficulty, ask your course instructor to assist you in applying these techniques.

CEILING SHOT RETURN

The backhand ceiling shot return can be used when the lob serve to the backhand side bounces off the back wall high, well above your waist. It is hit with the same technique as for the backhand ceiling shot you learned earlier, with the contact point about head-high. The objective is to hit this shot to either corner, moving the server well out of the control zone. Once vacated, you can take over the control zone.

INSTRUCTOR DEMONSTRATION

Your course instructor will explain and demonstrate the key performance cues for the ceiling shot return from a lob serve to the backhand side. If you have questions, be sure to ask them before proceeding to the individualized task sequence. Refer to Illustration 8.9 as your instructor explains and demonstrates each performance cue for this skill

READINESS DRILL

8-9.   Find a partner and make sure both of you are wearing eyeguards. You will stand in the proper position for receiving serves (R). Your partner makes a lob serve to your backhand side (about head-high for you) and moves to the middle of the control zone (refer to Illustration 8.9). Move into position and return this serve with a ceiling shot. The ball should rebound so that it forces the server to move deep into one of the corners. **The serving partner should not attempt to hit your return shot; he or she should move into the control zone, and then track the ball into the corner.** Practice this drill until you have hit 20 successful shots. Switch roles with your partner after every five attempts.

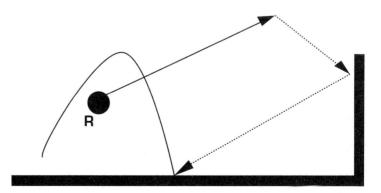

Illustration 8.9
Ceiling shot (side view)
from a lob serve

If you experience difficulty with the readiness drill, refer to the **performance cues** and review each cue as presented. If you still have difficulty, ask your course instructor to assist you in applying these techniques.

LEARNING TIPS

1. Use a variety of returns. Generally, if the serve generates a *setup* (an errant serve), then a kill shot or V-pass is recommended.
2. Do not drift too close to the side wall when tracking the lob serve. If you do, you are likely to strike the wall with the racquet before hitting the ball. This is one of the strategic objectives when making the lob serve, so don't get "suckered" into that mistake.
3. If you are forced to contact the ball above your waist, a ceiling ball is the recommended return.
4. Don't underestimate the value of a ceiling shot return of serve. A well-executed ceiling shot will force the server from the control position and allow you ample time to relocate your court position into that area.

Common Errors and Their Correction

Error	Correction
Return of serve lacks power.	Improved footwork and reading the walls will allow you to set up for the return of serve.
Return of serve provides the server with an easy kill shot.	1. Use a variety of service returns. 2. Be aggressive when the serve does not pressure you.
You drift too close to the side wall and hit the wall before the ball.	1. The lob serve allows you plenty of time to get to the wall and set up properly; get there quickly and keep a safe arm's length from the side wall on setup. 2. Be decisive in making your return shot so that the wall is not a factor on the swing.

CHALLENGE TASK

Serving

Find another student who has also completed Readiness Drill 8-9. Be sure both of you are wearing your eyeguards. This game is limited only to serving and returning serves. **Do not begin a rally at any time, since your partner will not be prepared.** On turn, the server attempts any serve she or he wishes, delivered under all the applicable rules. *The objective for the server* is to hit a serve that can't be returned by the receiver, or the return does not force the server out of the control zone. *The objective for the receiver* is to hit a return that the server cannot handle or that forces the server out of the control zone.

Alternate with your partner as server and receiver for 10 rounds. The scoring for each serve goes like this:

Result	Point(s)	Awarded to
Any fault by server	1	Receiver
Ace serve (legal serve, untouched by receiver)	2	Server
Fault on return of legal serve	1	Server
Return handled (hit legally to front wall) by server in control cone	1	Server
Return forces server out of the control zone	1	Receiver
Ace return (legal, and cannot be touched by the server on one bounce)	2	Receiver

The game is won by the player with the most points after 10 rounds. Repeat this challenge task with one player 3 times, and then challenge several other players in the class.

MODULE **9**

PASSING AND KILL SHOTS

INTRODUCTION

In the most simple terms, the main object in racquetball is to hit a shot that your opponent cannot legally return before the ball bounces on the court twice. At times you must hit a defensive shot that allows you to "stay in the point" long enough to get an opportunity for an offensive shot. Midwall drives and ceiling shots are usually defensive shots, used to move the opponent out of the control zone, but are not likely to lead directly to a point or a handout. Offensive shots are those made with the immediate goal of "putting the opponent away" and preventing any kind of return by him or her. During a rally you should look for any opportunity to be aggressive and hit an offensive shot—before your opponent gets the chance to hit an offensive shot at you. There are two basic offensive shots in racquetball: **passing shots** and **kill shots**. Each type has a few variations that you will learn in this module.

PASSING SHOTS

A passing shot is an offensive stroke that is designed to end the rally "right now," or at least to elicit a weak return from your opponent. **Cross-court passing shots** are hit from either the forehand or backhand side when your opponent has taken a position forward of the control position. Passing shots can also be used to force your opponent to chase around the court to retrieve the ball. Some players use this stroke to attempt to fatigue their opponent and therefore gain an edge in the match. An **up-the-wall passing shot** is used when your opponent is positioned in the control zone, shaded to the side opposite where you are positioned on the court.

The key to making passing shots is to understand your opponent's court position in relationship to your own. In some ways, the decision is made for you; all you need to do is recognize the situation at the moment you prepare to make your shot.

Opponent's Position	Your Position	Hit
In front of CZ	Left of CZ	Backhand cross-court pass
In front of CZ	Right of CZ	Forehand cross-court pass
Shaded to the right in CZ	Behind and left of CZ	Backhand up-the-wall pass
Shaded to the left in CZ	Behind and right of CZ	Forehand up-the-wall pass
Behind CZ (anywhere)	Lateral to or in front of opponent	Kill shot

CZ = control zone.

INSTRUCTOR DEMONSTRATION

Your course instructor will explain and demonstrate the key performance cues for the **forehand cross-court passing shot**. As you will note, this shot uses the same technique as the forehand drive shot, with the contact point about knee-high. If you have questions, be sure to ask them before proceeding to the individualized task sequence. Refer to Illustration 9.1 as your instructor explains and demonstrates each performance cue for this skill

READINESS DRILL

9-1.   Find a partner and make sure both of you are wearing eyeguards. You will stand about 10 feet behind the receiving line, one step to the right of center (R). Your partner (P) stands between the short line and the receiving line and makes a medium-paced drive serve to your forehand side (about knee-high) and assumes a ready position **looking toward the front wall** (refer to Illustration 9.1). Move into position and return

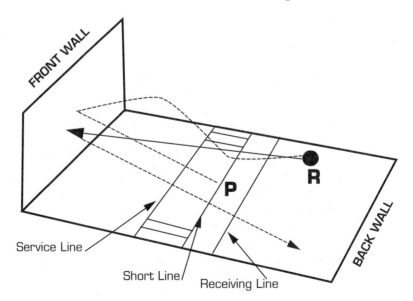

Illustration 9.1
Forehand cross-court passing shot

Service Line

Short Line

Receiving Line

this serve with a forehand cross-court passing shot. The ball should rebound so that it passes more than an arm length to the left of your partner, no more than shoulder-high to him or her. **Your partner should not attempt to return your shot; he or she is there only to help you gauge the accuracy of your shot.** Practice this drill until you have hit 20 successful shots. Switch roles with your partner after every five attempts.

If you experience difficulty with the readiness drill, refer to the **performance cues** and review each cue as presented. If you still have difficulty, ask your course instructor to assist you in applying these techniques.

INSTRUCTOR DEMONSTRATION

Your course instructor will explain and demonstrate the key performance cues for the **backhand cross-court passing shot**. As you will note, this shot uses the same technique as the backhand drive shot, with the contact point about knee-high. If you have questions, be sure to ask them before proceeding to the individualized task sequence. Refer to Illustration 9.2 as your instructor explains and demonstrates each performance cue for this skill.

READINESS DRILL

9-2.   Find a partner and make sure both of you are wearing eyeguards. You will stand about 10 feet behind the receiving line, one step to the left of center (R). Your partner (P) stands between the short line and the receiving line and makes a medium-paced drive serve to your back-

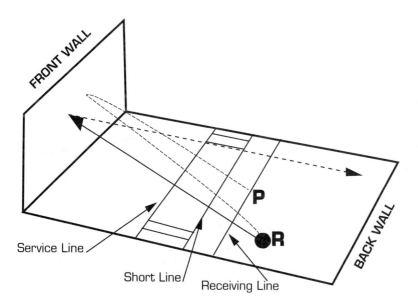

Service Line

Short Line

Receiving Line

Illustration 9.2
Backhand cross-court passing shot

hand side (about knee-high) and assumes a ready position **looking toward the front wall** (refer to Illustration 9.2). Move into position and return this serve with a backhand cross-court passing shot. The ball should rebound so that it passes more than an arm length to the right of your partner, no more than shoulder-high to him or her. **Your partner should not attempt to return your shot; he or she is there only to help you gauge the accuracy of your shot**. Practice this drill until you have hit 20 successful shots. Switch roles with your partner after every five attempts.

If you experience difficulty with the readiness drill, refer to the **performance cues** and review each cue as presented. If you still have difficulty, ask your course instructor to assist you in applying these techniques.

INSTRUCTOR DEMONSTRATION

Your course instructor will explain and demonstre the key performance cue-for the **forehand up-the-wall passing shot**. As you will note, this shot uses the same technique as the forehand drive shot, with the contact point about knee-high. If you have questions, be sure to ask them before proceeding to the individualized task sequence. Refer to Illustration 9.3 as your instructor explains and demonstrates each performance cue for this skill.

READINESS DRILL

9-3.   Find a partner and make sure both of you are wearing eyeguards. You will stand just in front of the receiving line, one step to the right of

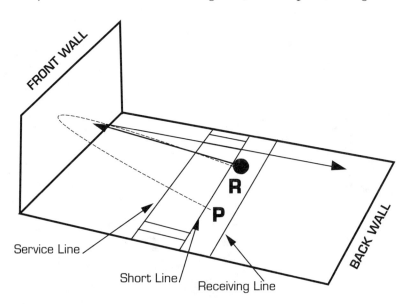

Illustration 9.3
Forehand up-the-
wall passing shot

center (R). Your partner (P) stands between the short line and the receiving line on the left side and makes a medium-paced drive serve to your forehand side (about knee-high) (refer back to Illustration 9.3). Return this serve with a forehand up-the-wall passing shot. The ball should rebound so that it passes between you and the right side wall, no more than shoulder-high to you. The ball cannot hit a side wall on the way to the back wall. **Your partner should not attempt to return your shot.** Practice this drill until you have hit 20 successful shots. Switch roles with your partner after every five attempts.

If you experience difficulty with the readiness drill, refer to the **performance cues** and review each cue as presented. If you still have difficulty, ask your course instructor to assist you in applying these techniques.

INSTRUCTOR DEMONSTRATION

Your course instructor will explain and demonstrate the key performance cues for the **backhand up-the-wall passing shot.** As you will note, this shot uses the same technique as the backhand drive shot, with the contact point about knee-high. If you have questions, be sure to ask them before proceeding to the individualized task sequence. Refer to Illustration 9.4 as your instructor explains and demonstrates each performance cue for this skill.

READINESS DRILL

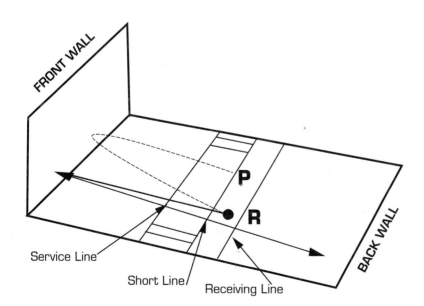

Service Line

Short Line

Receiving Line

Illustration 9.4
Backhand up-the-wall passing shot

9-4. Find a partner and make sure both of you are wearing eyeguards. You will stand just in front of the receiving line, one step to the left of center (R). Your partner (P) stands between the short line and the receiving line on the right side and makes a medium-paced drive serve to your backhand side (about knee-high) (refer to Illustration 9.4). Return this serve with a backhand up-the-wall passing shot. The ball should rebound so that it passes between you and the left side wall, no more than shoulder-high to you. The ball cannot hit a side wall on the way to the back wall. **Your partner should not attempt to return your shot.** Practice this drill until you have hit 20 successful shots. Switch roles with your partner after every five attempts.

If you experience difficulty with the readiness drill, refer to the **performance cues** and review each cue as presented. If you still have difficulty, ask your course instructor to assist you in applying these techniques.

LEARNING TIPS

1. As you see the ball rebound from the front wall, quickly move into position to execute a passing shot.
2. To hit a cross-court shot, the point of contact is adjusted forward of the midline of the body.
3. Be aggressive; attempt to pass your opponent with a high-velocity shot.
4. Be decisive with your shot selection

Common Errors and Their Correction

Error	Correction
Passing shot lacks power.	Use your body weight transfer and hip and shoulder rotation to increase the velocity of your stroke.
Incorrect angle of passing shot.	Adjust your target area on the front wall in relation to opponent's position.
Your passing shots get returned often.	1. Be decisive when making your shot choice. 2. Be aggressive with the shot once you have made your choice.

KILL SHOTS

The kill shot is designed to end the rally immediately. The ball contacts the front wall within a few inches up from the floor, assuring that the rebound from the wall will be extremely low and almost impossible to return. The perfect kill shot contacts the front wall so low that it rolls back into the court without any bounces. This is called a *roll out*. There are two popular variations of the kill shot. The *straight kill shot* does not use the side walls. The *pinch kill* utilizes the side & front wall combination.

INSTRUCTOR DEMONSTRATION

Your course instructor will explain and demonstrate the key performance cues for the **forehand straight kill shot**. As you will note, this shot uses the same technique as for the forehand drive shot, with the contact point very low to the court, well below the knee. If you have questions, be sure to ask them before proceeding to the individualized task sequence. Refer to Illustration 9.5 as your instructor explains and demonstrates each performance cue for this skill

READINESS DRILL

9-5. Mark a rectangle on the front wall. The top of the rectangle should be 18 inches from the court; the left side should be 8 feet from the right wall (see Illustration 9.5). Take a position **on the receiving line** to the

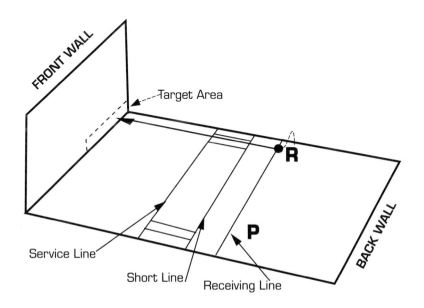

Illustration 9.5
Forehand straight kill shot

right of the court (R). Drop a ball to the court as to hit a forehand drive. On the first bounce of the ball, execute a forehand kill shot (**straight kill**) aimed at the front wall. The trajectory of the ball should be low and parallel to the floor. The ball should strike the front wall within 18 inches from court level. **Hit 5 of these kill shots.** Move back from the receiving line a few feet and repeat this drill. **Hit 5 kill shots from this court position.**

If you experience difficulty with the readiness drill, refer to the **performance cues** and review each cue as presented. If you still have difficulty, ask your course instructor to assist you in applying these techniques.

LEARNING TIPS (for all Kill Shots)

1. Move into position quickly so that you let the ball drop to the proper elevation.
2. Do not reach for the ball; this can cause the ball to be hit higher than intended and provide an easy return for your opponent.
3. Step to your target with the nondominant foot.
4. Contact with the ball must be low to the floor.
5. Flatten out your stroke to assure a level swing.

Common Errors and Their Correction

Error	Correction
Kill shot lacks power.	Use your body weight transfer and hip and shoulder rotation to increase the velocity of your stroke.
Ball contacts front wall too high.	1. Contact the ball closer to the floor. 2. Do not reach; let the ball come to you. 3. Stroke the ball with a flatter swing. 4. Lower your follow-through.

CRITERION TASK 9-1

Forehand Straight Kill Shot: Partner-Checked

Find a partner for this task. Be sure that both of you are wearing your eye-guards. Mark a rectangle on the front wall. The top of the rectangle should be 18 inches from the court, the left side should be 8 feet from the right wall (refer to Illustration 9.5). Take a position **on the receiving line** to the right of the court. Your partner will be just behind the receiving line, on the far left side of the court (P). She or he will hit a low drive shot off the front wall to your forehand side. Move into position and return this with a forehand kill shot (**straight kill**) aimed at the front wall.

To be counted as successful, your shot must strike the front wall first, within the defined rectangular target, and not hit the side wall until it has passed you on the rebound. Practice this task in blocks of 10 shots. Try to hit every shot that comes to you. If your partner's shot to you cannot be hit with a forehand kill shot, do not count that one. Record the number of successful shots for each block on the **Personal Recording Form**. When three block scores reach or exceed 7 out of 10, have your partner initial and date in the space provided.

Personal Recording Form									
Block 1	Block 2	Block 3	Block 4	Block 5	Block 6	Block 7	Block 8	Block 9	Block 10
__/10	__/10	__/10	__/10	__/10	__/10	__/10	__/10	__/10	__/10

Your partner's initials _____   Date completed _____

INSTRUCTOR DEMONSTRATION

Your course instructor will explain and demonstrate the key performance cues for the **forehand pinch kill shot to the right corner**. As you will note, this shot uses the same technique as for the straight shot, with the contact point very low to the court, well below the knee. The major difference is that you

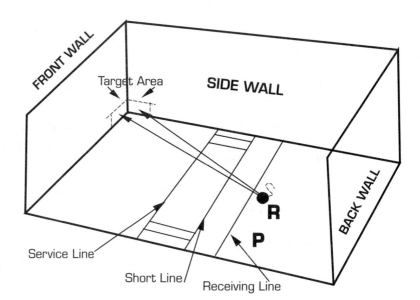

Illustration 9.6
Forehand pinch kill
(right side)

are trying to hit very low to the right front corner of the court. If you have questions, be sure to ask them before proceeding to the individualized task sequence. Refer to Illustration 9.6 as your instructor explains and demonstrates each performance cue for this skill

READINESS DRILL

9-6. Mark a rectangle on the right of the front wall and the right side wall. The top of the rectangle should be 18 inches from the court, extending from the corner crotch 3 feet on both walls (see Illustration 9.6). Take a position **just behind the receiving line** in the center of the court (R). Drop a ball to the court as to hit a forehand drive. On the first bounce of the ball, execute a forehand pinch kill shot aimed at the right corner of the front wall. The trajectory of the ball should be low and parallel to the floor. The ball should strike the front wall or side wall first, hitting in the rectangular target. **Hit 5 of these kill shots.** Move back from the receiving line a few feet and repeat this drill. **Hit 5 kill shots from this court position.**

If you experience difficulty with the readiness drill, refer to the **performance cues** and review each cue as presented. If you still have difficulty, ask your course instructor to assist you in applying these techniques.

CRITERION TASK 9-2

Forehand Pinch Kill Shot to the Right Corner: Partner-Checked

Find a partner for this task. Be sure that both of you are wearing your eye-guards. Mark a rectangle on the front wall and right side wall. The top of the rectangle should be 18 inches from the court, extending from the corner crotch 3 feet on both walls (refer to Illustration 9.6). Take a position **just behind the receiving line** in the center of the court (R). Your partner will be just behind the receiving line, on the far left side of the court (P). She or he will hit a low drive shot off the front wall to your forehand side. Move into position and return this with a forehand pinch kill shot aimed at the right corner of the front wall.

To be counted as successful, your shot must strike either wall first and then the other wall, *both times* within the defined rectangular target. Practice this task in blocks of 10 shots. Try to hit every shot that comes to you. If your partner's shot to you cannot be hit with a forehand pinch kill shot, do not count that one. Record the number of successful shots for each block on the **Personal Recording Form**. When three block scores reach or exceed 6 out of 10, have your partner initial and date in the space provided.

Personal Recording Form									
Block 1	Block 2	Block 3	Block 4	Block 5	Block 6	Block 7	Block 8	Block 9	Block 10
___/10	___/10	___/10	___/10	___/10	___/10	___/10	___/10	___/10	___/10

Your partner's initials _____ Date completed _____

INSTRUCTOR DEMONSTRATION

Your course instructor will explainn and demonstrate the key performance cues for the **forehand pinch kill shot to the left corner**. As you will note, this shot uses the same technique as for the straight shot, with the contact point very low to the court, well below the knee. The major difference is that you are trying to hit very low to the left front corner of the court. If you have questions, be sure to ask them before proceeding to the individualized task sequence. Refer to Illustration 9.7 as your instructor explains and demonstrates each performance cue for this skill

READINESS DRILL

9-7.   Mark a rectangle on the left of the front wall and the left side wall. The top of the rectangle should be 18 inches from the court, extending from the corner crotch 3 feet on both walls (see Illustration 9.7). Take a position **just behind the receiving line** two steps to the right of center (R). Drop a ball to the court as to hit a forehand drive. On the first bounce of the ball, execute a forehand pinch kill shot aimed at the left corner of the front wall. The trajectory of the ball should be low and parallel to the floor. The ball should strike the front wall or side wall first, hitting in the rectangular target. **Hit 5 of these kill shots.** Move back from the receiving line a few feet and repeat this drill. **Hit 5 kill shots from this court position.**

If you experience difficulty with the readiness drill, refer to the **performance cues** and review each cue as presented. If you still have difficulty, ask your course instructor to assist you in applying these techniques.

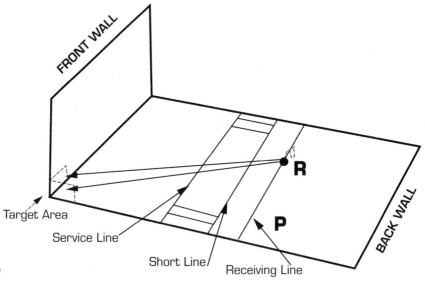

Illustration 9.7
Forehand pinch kill
(left side)

CRITERION TASK 9-3

Forehand Pinch Kill Shot to the Left Corner: Partner-Checked

Find a partner for this task. Be sure that both of you are wearing eyeguards. Mark a rectangle on the front wall and left side wall. The top of the rectangle should be 18 inches from the court, extending from the corner crotch 3 feet on both walls (refer to Illustration 9.7). Take a position just behind the receiving line two steps to the right of center (R). Your partner will be just behind the receiving line, on the far left side of the court (P). She or he will hit a low drive shot off the front wall to your forehand side. Move into position and return this with a forehand pinch kill shot aimed at the left corner of the front wall.

To be counted as successful, your shot must strike either wall first and then the other wall, both times within the defined rectangular target. Practice this task in blocks of 10 shots. Try to hit every shot that comes to you. If your partner's shot to you cannot be hit with a forehand pinch kill shot, do not count that one. Record the number of successful shots for each block on the **Personal Recording Form**. When three block scores reach or exceed 6 out of 10, have your partner initial and date in the space provided.

Personal Recording Form									
Block 1	Block 2	Block 3	Block 4	Block 5	Block 6	Block 7	Block 8	Block 9	Block 10
__/10	__/10	__/10	__/10	__/10	__/10	__/10	__/10	__/10	__/10

Your partner's initials _____ Date completed _____

RACQUETBALL RULES AND GAME STRATEGY

READING ASSIGNMENT

Take time to carefully read the following Rules of Racquetball and the section on racquetball strategy. As you read, make marginal notes on those items that are not clear to you. The next day in class ask your instructor to provide a longer explanation of these items or, better yet, a *demonstration*. Many of the rules and strategies can be best understood by seeing and hearing how they are interpreted and applied.

When you have finished the reading and have no more questions for your instructor, complete the brief Racquetball Knowledge Quiz at the back of this module. If the quiz will be used for grading, your instructor will inform you about how it will be evaluated. If this quiz will not be used for grading, we recommend that you score at least 80% **and** have your instructor review missed answers with you. In this way, you will have a good working knowledge of racquetball rules and strategy before you begin competitive play in class or on your own.

OFFICIAL RULES OF RACQUETBALL

Reprinted with permission of the United States Racquetball Association.

TYPES OF GAMES

Racquetball may be played by two, or four players. When played by two it is called singles and when played by four, doubles. A nontournament variation of the game is played by three players, called cutthroat.

POINTS AND OUTS

Points are scored only by the serving side when it serves an *ace* (an irretrievable serve) or wins a rally. Losing the serve is called an *out* in singles. In doubles, when the first server loses serve, it is called a *hand out* and when the second server loses the serve it is a *side out*.

MATCH, GAME, TIE BREAKER

A match is won by the first side winning two games. The first two games of a match are played to 15 points. In the event that each side wins one game, the tie breaker game is played to 11 points.

COURTS AND EQUIPMENT

COURTS

The specifications for the standard four-wall racquetball court are as follows:

(a) Dimensions. The dimensions shall be 20 feet wide, 40 feet long, and 20 feet high with a back wall at least 12 feet high. All surfaces shall be in play, with the exception of any gallery opening or surfaces designated as court hinders.

(b) Lines and zones. Racquetball courts shall be divided and marked with lines 1 inch wide as follows:

1. **Short line.** The back edge of the short line is midway between and is parallel to the front and back walls.
2. **Service line.** The front edge of the service line is parallel with and 5 feet in front of the back edge of the short line.
3. **Service zone.** The service zone is the 5-foot area between the outer edges of the short line and service line.
4. **Service boxes.** The service boxes are located at each end of the service zone and are designated by lines parallel to the side wall. The edge of the line nearest to the center of the court shall be 18 inches from the nearest side wall.
5. **Drive serve lines.** The drive serve lines, which form the drive serve zone, are parallel to the side wall and are within the service zone. The edge of the line nearest to the center of the court shall be 3 feet from the nearest side wall.
6. **Receiving line.** The receiving line is a broken line parallel to the short line. The back edge of the receiving line is 5 feet from the back edge of the short line. The receiving line begins with a line 21 inches long that extends from each side wall; the two lines are connected by an alternating series of 6-inch spaces and 6-inch lines (17 6-inch spaces and 16 6-inch lines).
7. **Safety zone.** The safety zone is the 5-foot area bounded by the back edges of the short line and the receiving line. The zone is observed only during the serve.

RACQUET SPECIFICATIONS

(a) The racquet, including bumper guard and all solid parts of the handle, may not exceed 21 inches in length.

(b) The racquet frame may be of any material judged to be safe.

(c) The racquet frame must include a thong that must be securely attached to the player's wrist.

APPAREL

(a) Lensed eyewear required. Lensed eyewear designed for racquet sports is required apparel for all players. The protective eyewear must be worn as designed and may not be altered. Players who require corrective eyewear also must wear lensed eyewear designed for racquet sports.

THE GAME

SERVE

The player or team winning the coin toss has the option to serve or receive for the start of the first game. The second game will begin in reverse order of the first game. The player or team scoring the highest total of points in games 1 and 2 will have the option to serve or receive first at the start of the tie breaker. In the event that both players or teams score an equal number of points in the first two games, another coin toss will take place and the winner of the toss will have the option to serve or receive.

START

The serve is started from any place within the service zone. Neither the ball nor any part of either foot may extend beyond either line of the service zone when initiating the service motion. Stepping on, but not over, the lines is permitted. When completing the service motion, the server may step over the service (front) line provided that some part of both feet remain on or inside the line until the served ball passes the short line. The server may not step over the short line until the ball passes the short line.

MANNER

Once the service motion begins, the ball must be bounced on the floor in the zone and be struck by the racquet before it bounces a second time. After being struck, the ball must hit the front wall first and on the rebound hit the floor behind the back edge of the short line, either with or without touching one of the side walls.

SERVE IN DOUBLES

(a) Order of serve. Each team shall inform the referee of the order of serve that shall be followed throughout that game. The order of serve may be changed between games. At the beginning of each game, when the first server of the first team to serve is out, the team is out. Thereafter, both players on each team shall serve until the team receives a hand out and a side out.

(b) Partner's position. On each serve, the server's partner shall stand erect with back to the side wall and with both feet on the floor within the service box from the moment the server begins service motion until the served ball passes the short line. Violations are called *foot faults*. However, if the server's partner enters the safety zone before the ball passes the short line, the server loses service.

DEFECTIVE SERVES

Defective serves are of three types, resulting in penalties as follows:

(a) Dead-ball serve. A dead-ball serve results in no penalty and the server is given another serve (without canceling a prior fault serve).

(b) Fault serve. Two fault serves result in a hand out.

(c) Out serve. An out serve results in a hand out.

DEAD-BALL SERVE

Dead-ball serves do not cancel any previous fault serve. The following are dead-ball serves:

(a) Ball Hits Partner. A serve that strikes the server's partner while in the doubles box is a dead-ball serve. A serve that touches the floor before touching the server's partner is a short serve.

(b) Court hinders. A serve that takes an irregular bounce because it hit a wet spot or an irregular surface on the court is a dead-ball serve, also is any serve that hits any surface designated by local rules as an obstruction.

(c) Broken ball. If the ball is determined to have broken on the serve, a new ball shall be substituted and the serve shall be replayed, not canceling any prior fault serve.

FAULT SERVES

The following serves are faults and any two in succession result in an out:

(a) Foot faults. A foot fault results when:

1. The server does not begin the service motion with both feet in the service zone.

2. The server steps completely over the service line (no part of the foot on or inside the service zone) before the served ball crosses the short line.
3. In doubles, the server's partner is not in the service box with both feet on the floor and back to the wall from the time the server begins the service motion until the ball passes the short line.

(b) Short service. A short serve is any served ball that first hits the front wall and, on the rebound, hits the floor on or in front of the short line (with or without touching a side wall).

(c) Three-wall serve. A three-wall serve is any served ball that first hits the front wall and, on the rebound, strikes both side walls before touching the floor.

(d) Ceiling serve. A ceiling serve is any served ball that first hits the front wall and then touches the ceiling (with or without touching a side wall).

(e) Long serve. A long serve is a served ball that first hits the front wall and rebounds to the back wall before touching the floor (with or without touching a side wall).

(f) Out-of-court serve. An out-of-court serve is any served ball that first hits the wall and, before striking the floor, goes out of the court.

(g) Bouncing ball outside service zone. Bouncing the ball outside the service zone as a part of the service motion is a fault serve.

(h) Illegal drive serve. A drive serve in which the player fails to observe the 17-foot drive service zone (the receiving line).

(i) Screen serve. A served ball that first hits the front wall and on the rebound passes so closely to the server, or server's partner in doubles, that it prevents the receiver from having a clear view of the ball. (The receiver is obligated to place himself in good court position, near center court, to obtain this view.) The screen serve is the only fault serve that may not be appealed.

OUT SERVES

Any of the following serves results in an out:

(a) Two consecutive fault serves

(b) Missed serve attempt. Any attempt to strike the ball that results in a total miss or in the ball touching any part of the server's body. Also, allowing the ball to bounce more than once during the service motion.

(c) Touched serve. Any served ball that on the rebound from the front wall touches the server or server's racquet, or any ball intentionally stopped or caught by the server or server's partner.

(d) Fake or balk serve. Any movement of the racquet toward the ball during the serve that is noncontinuous and done for the purpose of deceiving the receiver. If a balk serve occurs, but the referee believes that no deceit was involved, he has the option of declaring "no serve" and have-ing the serve replayed without penalty.

(e) **Illegal hit.** An illegal hit includes contacting the ball twice, carrying the ball, or hitting the ball with the handle of the racquet or part of the body or uniform.

(f) **Non-front wall serve.** Any served ball that does not strike the front wall first.

(g) **Crotch serve.** Any served ball that hits the crotch of the front wall and floor, front wall and side wall, or front wall and ceiling is an out serve (because it did not hit the front wall first). A serve into the crotch of the back wall and floor is a good serve and in play. A served ball that hits the crotch of the side wall and the floor behind the short line is in play.

(h) **Out-of-order serve.** In doubles, when either partner serves out of order, the points scored by that server will be subtracted and an out serve will be called; if the second server serves out of order, the out serve will be applied to the first server and the second server will resume serving. If the player designated as the first server serves out of order, a side out will be called. In a match with line judges, the referee may enlist their aid to recall the number of points scored out of order.

(i) **Ball hits partner.** A served ball that hits the doubles partner while out-side the doubles box results in loss of serve.

(j) **Safety zone violation.** If the server, or doubles partner, enters into the safety zone before the served ball passes the short line, it shall result in the loss of serve.

RETURN OF SERVE

(a) **Receiving Position**

1. The receiver may not enter the safety zone until the ball bounces or crosses the receiving line.
2. On the fly return attempt, the receiver may not strike the ball until the ball breaks the plane of the receiving line. The receiver's follow-through may carry the receiver or his racquet past the receiving line.
3. Neither the receiver nor his racquet may break the plane of the short line, except if the ball is struck after rebounding off the back wall.
4. Any violation by the receiver results in a point for the server.

(a) **Defective serve.** A player on the receiving side may not intentionally catch or touch a served ball (such as an apparently long or short serve) until the referee has made a call or the ball has touched the floor for a sec-ond time. Violation results in a point.

(b) **Legal return.** After a legal serve, a player on the receiving team must strike the ball on the fly or after the first bounce, before the ball touches the floor the second time; and return the ball to the front wall, either directly or after touching one or both side walls, the back wall, or the ceiling, or any combination of these surfaces. A returned ball must touch the front wall before touching the floor.

(c) **Failure to return.** The failure to return a serve results in a point for the server.

CHANGES OF SERVE

(a) **Outs.** A server is entitled to continue serving until one of the following occurs:

1. **Out serve**
2, **Two consecutive fault serves**
3. **Ball hits artner.** Player hits partner with attempted return.
4. **Failure to return ball.** Player, or partner, fails to keep the ball in play.
5. **Avoidable hinder.** Player or partner commits an avoidable hinder that results in an out.

(b) **Side out.** In singles, retiring the server is a side out. In doubles, the side is retired when both partners have lost service, except that the team that serves first at the beginning of each game loses serve when the first server is retired.

(c) **Effect of sideout.** When the server (or the serving team) receives a side-out, the server becomes the receiver and the receiver becomes the server.

RALLIES

All play that occurs after the successful return of serve is called the *rally*. Play shall be conducted according to the following rules:

(a) **Legal hits.** Only the head of the racquet may be used at any time to return the ball. The racquet may be held in one or both hands. Switching hands to hit a ball, touching the ball with any part of the body or uniform, or removing the wrist thong results in a loss of the rally.

(b) **One touch.** The player or team trying to return the ball may touch or strike the ball only once or else the rally is lost. The ball may not be carried. (A carried ball is one that rests on the racquet in such a way that the effect is more of a sling or throw than a hit.)

(c) **Failure to return.** Any of the following constitutes a failure to make a legal return during a rally:

1. The ball bounces on the floor more than once before being hit.
2. The ball does not reach the front wall on the fly.
3. The ball caroms off a player's racquet into a gallery or wall opening without first hitting the front wall.
4. A ball that obviously did not have the velocity or direction to hit the front wall strikes another player on the court.

5. A ball struck by one player on a team hits the player or his or her partner.
6. Committing a point hinder.
7. Switching hands during a rally.
8. Failure to use wrist thong on racquet.
9. Touching the ball with the body or uniform.
10. Carrying or slinging the ball with the racquet.

(d) **Effect of failure to return.** Violations of rules (a), (b) or (c) above result in a loss of rally. If the serving player or team loses the rally, it is an out (hand out or side out). If the receiver loses the rally, it results in a point for the server.

(e) **Return attempts**

1. In singles, if a player swings at the ball and misses it, the player may continue to attempt to return the ball until it touches the floor for the second time.
2. In doubles, if one player swings at the ball and misses it, both partners may make further attempts to return the ball until it touches the floor the second time. Both partners on a side are entitled to return the ball.

(f) **Out-of-court ball**

1. **After return.** Any ball returned to the front wall that, on the rebound or the first bounce, goes into the gallery or through any opening in a sidewall shall be declared dead and the server shall receive two serves.
2. **No return.** Any ball not returned to the front wall, but which caroms off a player's racquet into the gallery or into any opening in a side wall either with or without touching the ceiling, side wall, or back wall, shall be an out for the player failing to make the return or a point for the opponent.

(g) **Broken ball.** If there is any suspicion that a ball has broken during a rally, play shall continue until the end of the rally. The referee or any player may request that the ball be examined. If the referee decides the ball is broken, the ball will be replaced and the rally replayed. The server will get two serves. The only proper way to check for a broken ball is to squeeze it (checking the ball by striking it with a racquet will not be considered a valid check).

(h) **Play stoppage**

1. If a foreign object enters the court or any other outside interference occurs, the referee shall stop the play.
2. If a player loses a shoe or other properly worn equipment, the referee shall stop the play if the occurrence interferes with ensuing play or player's safety; however, safety permitting, the offensive player is entitled to one opportunity to hit a rally ending shot.

(i) **Replays.** Whenever a rally is replayed for any reason, the server is awarded two serves. A previous fault serve is not considered.

DEAD-BALL HINDERS

A rally is replayed without penalty and the server receives two serves whenever a dead-ball hinder occurs.

(a) Situations

1. **Court hinders.** The referee should stop play immediately whenever the ball hits any part of the court that was designated in advance as a court hinder (such as a door handle). The referee should also stop play (i) when the ball takes an irregular bounce as a result of contacting a rough surface (such as court light or vent) or after striking a wet spot on the floor or wall and (ii) when, in the referee's opinion, the irregular bounce affected the rally. A court hinder is the only type of hinder that is appealable.

2. **Ball hits opponent.** When an opponent is hit by a return shot in flight, it is a dead-ball hinder. If the opponent is struck by a ball that obviously did not have the velocity or direction to reach the front wall, it is not a hinder, and the player that hit the ball will lose the rally. A player who has been hit by the ball can stop play and make the call, though the call must be made immediately and acknowledged by the referee.

3. **Body Contact.** If body contact occurs that the referee believes was sufficient to stop the rally, either for the purpose of preventing injury by further contact or because the contact prevented a player from being able to make a reasonable return, the referee shall call a hinder. Incidental body contact in which the offensive player clearly will have the advantage should not be called a hinder, unless the offensive player obviously stops play. Contact with the racquet on the follow-through normally is not considered a dead-ball hinder.

4. **Screen ball.** Any ball rebounding from the front wall so close to the body of the defensive team that it interferes with or prevents the offensive player from having clear view of the ball. A ball that passes between the legs of the side that just returned the ball is not automatically a screen. It depends on the proximity of the players. Again, the call should work to the advantage of the offensive player.

5. **Backswing hinder.** Any body or racquet contact, on the backswing or en route to or just prior to returning the ball, that impairs the hitter's ability to take a reasonable swing. This call can be made by the player attempting the return, though the call must be made immediately and is subject to the referee's approval. Note that the interference may be considered an avoidable hinder.

6. **Safety holdup.** Any player about to execute a return who believes that she or he is likely to strike the opponent with the ball or racquet may immediately stop play and request a dead-ball hinder. This call must be

made immediately and is subject to acceptance and approval by the referee. (The referee will grant a dead-ball hinder if he or she believes that the holdup was reasonable and the player would have been able to return the shot, and the referee may also call an avoidable hinder if warranted.)

7. **Other interference.** Any other unintentional interference that prevents an opponent from having a fair chance to see or return the ball, for example; when a ball from another court enters the court during a rally or when a referee's call on an adjacent court obviously distracts a player.

(b) **Effect of Hinders.** The referee's call of hinder stops play and voids any situation that follows, such as the ball hitting the player.

(c) **Avoidance.** While making an attempt to return the ball, a player is entitled to a fair chance to see and return the ball. It is the responsibility of the side that has just hit the ball to move so the receiving side may go straight to the ball and have an unobstructed view of the ball. In the judgment of the referee however, the receiver must make a reasonable effort to move toward the ball and have a reasonable chance to return the ball in order for a hinder to be called.

AVOIDABLE HINDERS

An avoidable hinder results in the loss of the rally. An avoidable hinder does not necessarily have to be an intentional act and is the result of any of the following:

(a) **Failure to move.** A player does not move sufficiently to allow an opponent a shot straight to the front wall as well as a cross-court shot which is a shot directly to the front wall at an angle that would cause the ball to rebound directly to the rear corner farthest from the player hitting the ball. Also when a player moves in such a direction that it prevents an opponent from taking either of these shots.

(b) **Stroke interference.** This occurs when a player moves, or fails to move, so that the opponent returning the ball does not have a free, unimpeded swing. This includes unintentionally moving in the wrong direction, which prevents an opponent from making an open offensive shot.

(c) **Blocking.** Moving into a position that blocks the opponent from getting to, or returning, the ball; or, in doubles, a player moves in front of an opponent as the player's partner is returning the ball.

(d) **Moving into the ball.** Moves in the way and is struck by the ball just played by the opponent.

(e) **Pushing.** Deliberately pushes or shoves opponent during a rally.

(f) **Intentional distractions.** Deliberate shouting, stamping of feet, waving of racquet, or any other manner of disrupting one's opponent.

(g) View obstruction. A player moves across an opponent's line of vision just before the opponent strikes the ball.

(h) Wetting the ball. The players, particularly the server, should ensure that the ball is dry prior to the serve. Any wet ball that is not corrected prior to the serve shall result in an avoidable hinder against the server.

(i) Equipment. The loss of any improperly worn equipment, or equipment not required on court, that interferes with the play of the ball or safety of the players is an avoidable hinder. Examples of this include the loss of improperly fastened eyewear and hand towels.

TIME-OUTS

(a) Rest periods. Each player or team is entitled to three 30-second time-outs in games to 15 points and two 30-second time-outs in games to 11 points. Timeouts may not be called by either side after service motion has begun. Calling for a time out when none remain or after service motion has begun or taking more than 30 seconds in a time-out, will result in the assessment of a technical for delay of game.

RACQUETBALL GAME STRATEGY

Congratulations! You have now completed all the Performance Skill and Knowledge Modules for PSIS racquetball. Having done so, you are well prepared to begin racquetball game play. Racquetball can be played in three versions: singles (one player versus one player), doubles (two-player teams), and cutthroat (three players on the court, with one player serving and two players defending, in rotation). Your instructor will explain each version to you and have you play each kind of game several times in class. At this point in your development, it is better to "play to learn" rather than "play to win." As you play your first several games, you should try to recognize and implement some common racquetball strategies that will help you become a more proficient player and faster.

Modern racquetball is a fast-paced game in which the ball moves around the court quickly and often unpredictably, at least for beginners who have not yet learned now to "read walls." Regardless of your skill level and experience, there are several basic strategies that apply in racquetball, whether you are playing singles, doubles, or cutthroat.

1. Racquetball is a territorial game. The player who can occupy the control zone longer will more likely win the rally. Therefore, you should hit shots that take your opponent(s) out of the control zone so that you may occupy it.
2. Make most of your serves to the backhand side, but every once in a while use a change-up to the forehand side with a strong drive serve or Z-serve. Do not lob serve to the forehand side.

3. Mix up the tempo of your serves and your use of drive, ceiling, and Z-serves. Even the best drive serves to the backhand side can be returned if they become predictable, allowing the receiver to "sit on them" by shading to that side and being ready.

4. Always look for opportunities to hit offensive shots. Do not pass up chances for passing shots and kill shots in a rally. You might not get another opportunity in that same rally.

5. Conversely, if you can't hit an offensive shot, try to hit a good defensive shot. Do not just "return the ball." If you can't attack, hit a shot that moves your opponent out of the control zone (preferably to the backhand side) and does not allow him or her to hit an attacking shot to you.

6. Move your opponent around the court. If your opponent is in the back of the court, hit a skill shot to the front. If your opponent is in the front, hit a passing shot or a ceiling shot. If your opponent is on one side, hit an up-the-wall passing or kill shot to the opposite side.

7. Be aggressive. Racquetball is not a game for timid players! Hit the ball hard whenever you can.

8. Search for weaknesses in your opponent's game. At the beginning of a match, try a variety of serves and shots to see how your opponent handles each type. If you detect a weakness on a certain serve or shot, make a mental note and come back to that serve or shot when you need to win a big point or side out. Do not "go to the well" too often; you are just giving your opponent more chances to practice that shot!

9. Never give up on a ball. The racquetball moves fast and takes long bounces; and with the back wall, it can actually bounce back in your direction. So, even if the ball gets by you, move quickly to get into position to play it again. Remember that the rules allow you to swing and miss and then swing again before the ball hits the court twice.

10. Do not hesitate to call hinders and screens when they affect your chance to play the ball. The racquetball court is small and so is the ball. It is not uncommon for one player to inadvertently get in the way of another player (hinder) or for one player to obstruct the view of another player (screen). With experience you will learn to recognize these situations and make fair calls, with no objections from your opponent.

RACQUETBALL KNOWLEDGE QUIZ

Name _____ Date _____

Circle the letter of the correct or best answer.

1. The player winning the coin toss has the option to
   A. serve   C. either A or B
   B. receive the serve

2. The server may not step over the short serve line until the ball rebounds from the front wall and
   A. passes over the service   C. strikes the floor of the receiving
      (front) line)   court
   B. passes over the short serve line D. is played by the receiver

3. A ceiling serve is termed a
   A. dead ball serve   C. fault serve
   B. side out   D. screen serve

4. A V-pass cross-court shot should be hit when you are near a side wall and your opponent is
   A. right in front of you   C. behind you
   B. in the center of the   D . In the back of the court
      control zone

5. Two consecutive fault serves result in a
   A. side out   C. point for the server
   B. point for the receiver

6. The score is 5 to 1. During the serve, the server allows the ball to bounce more than once during the serving motion. The score is now
   A. 1 to 5   C. 5 to 1
   B. 6 to 1   D. 5 to 2

7. Your (serving) opponent makes an errant drive serve to your forehand side, allowing you to attack. You should use a
   A. ceiling shot to his or   C. drive shot to his or her forehand
      her backhand   D. drive shot to his or her backhand
   B. kill shot

8. The score is 1–2. The receiver enters the safety zone before the served ball bounces in the receiving court. The score is now
   A. 1 to 2   C. 3 to 1
   B. 2 to 1   D. 1 to 3

9. The ball is coming to you about head-high, and you must play it right away. You should probably hit a
   A. kill shot   C. ceiling shot
   B. drive shot

10. The score is 10 to 7. During the next rally the ball touches the receiver's body as he or she returns the ball to the front wall. The score is now
    A. 7 to 10   C. 8 to 10
    B. 11 to 7   D. 10 to 7

11. You are the serve receiver. As the ball comes to you, the server obstructs your view of the oncoming ball, forcing you to miss it. You should call
    A. screen   C. hinder
    B fault   D. time out

12. The ball leaves the court on a serve. This is ruled a(n)
    A. side out   C. hinder
    B. out serve   D. fault

13. Any serve that does not hit the front wall first is ruled a(n)
    A. playable serve   C. out serve
    B. hand out   D. crotch serve

14. The served ball hits the doubles partner of the server while he or she is outside the service box. This results in
    A. loss of game   C. the point being replayed
    B. loss of serve   D. a time-out

15. In a doubles match the score is 10 to 11. The serve travels into the crotch of the back wall and floor and is not returned by the receiving team. The score is now
    A. 11 to 11   C. 11 to 10
    B. 10 to 11

16. The score is 0 to 6. During the next serve, the receiver hits the server with the service return. The score is now
    A. 1 to 6   C. 0 to 6
    B. 0 to 7   D. 6 to 0

17. Any violation by the serve receiver results in a
    A. replay   C. point for the receiver
    B. point for the server D. stoppage of play

18. The player who can occupy the _____ the
     longest is more likely to win a rally.
     A. serving area   C. front wall area
     B. back wall area   D. control zone

19. "Neutralizing the point" means that you
     A. hit a shot that can't be returned
     B. move your opponent out of the control zone with a shot
     C. are resting
     D. are going to call a hinder or screen

20. Your first objective during a rally is to
     A. move your opponent around the court
     B. save your energy for later points and games
     C. be patient and play cautiously
     D. be aggressive and attack whenever you can

Personal Progress Chart for PSIS Racquetball

Module	1	2	3	4	5	6	7	8	9	10	11	12	13	14	15
10 Racquetball Rules and Game Strategy															
9 Passing and Kill Shots															
8 Returning Serve															
7 Serving															
6 Ceiling shots															
5 Back wall Strokes															
4 Backhand Stroke															
3 Forehand Stroke															
2 Racquetball Basics															
1 Stretching															
Weeks in Class	1	2	3	4	5	6	7	8	9	10	11	12	13	14	15